The Winning Pitch

Jon Burnham

LONGWOOD
COMMUNICATIONS

Published by:
Longwood Communications
397 Kingslake Drive
DeBary, FL 32713
904-774-1991

Dedication

I dedicate this book to my wife, Bev. She is a blessing to me as a wife, to our children as a mother and to our grandchildren as a grandmother. Bev has inspired me for years to sit down and record the blessings the Lord has given me, as He has allowed me to watch other people come to Christ for salvation. She knew that these stories would encourage others to share their faith in Jesus.

Purpose

To encourage others to share their faith in Christ is the very purpose for writing this book. To God be the glory!

Contents

Acknowledgments

Dr. Walter Wilson was used to inspire me to follow his lead in sharing my faith with people the Lord brought my way. Dr. Wilson wrote several books explaining how God led him to witness. What was most interesting to me was how the Lord guided Dr. Wilson to bring spiritual matters into any conversation.

Dr. Bruce Dunn was used in a very unique way to humble me so that I learned how to get out of God's way and let Him do the work of reaching people for His Son's sake.

Dr. Bill Bright and Campus Crusade for Christ International were used to encourage me to memorize a way to share my faith in Christ. They showed Bev and me how to know what it really means to be filled, empowered and controlled by the Holy Spirit. Jay and Sandy Davis, the New Folk singing group and many others too numerous to mention were used of God in very special ways.

To all those who gave me permission to share their stories of salvation, wanting Jesus Christ to get the glory for changed lives.

One

THE WILD PITCH

A s a young boy I had a problem. I loved to throw rocks. Throwing was fun, but throwing at something was a lot more fun. Throwing a rock at something that would break increased the challenge. The crash had a special ring to it. When I broke a street light, I would run like crazy and scale a high fence with a single bound.

When I was about ten years old, I broke a street light and then had the audacity to brag about it within earshot of my mom. My big mouth and the accuracy of my right arm ended up costing me some big bucks for a fifth grader.

My mom grabbed me by the ear and marched me

up the street to the corner of Knoxville and Hanssler Place here in Peoria, Illinois. This was back in 1945 when we had electric-powered streetcars. As we waited for what seemed like hours for the next streetcar to arrive, did my mom let go of my ear? Why no! People would drive by, look and laugh. My pride was hurt more than my ear that had all the blood squeezed out of it. Mom's pinching fingers were powerful. She told me that I, too, could have strong hands and arms if I would pull weeds like she had done for years. She had a grip that wouldn't quit.

We got on the streetcar. Did my mom let go of my ear? No. It had become a part of her hand. At this point I don't think she would have known what to do without it. The streetcar conductor asked what was going on. I was hoping he would think my mom was taking me to the hospital to treat a wound to my ear. She set the record straight by announcing to him and everyone else on the streetcar that I had broken a street light and that she was taking me downtown to pay for it. After that announcement we sat down.

Did she let go of my ear? Absolutely not. I felt like all the blood in my system was being pumped into my head, but not one drop got to my ear.

The streetcar seemed to stop at every corner on the way downtown. At each corner people would get on. As they walked down the aisle to their seats, they saw this woman attached to my ear.

We finally got downtown. As we were getting off the streetcar, I looked around for some sympathetic glance from anyone. There was none. No one said, "Nice pitch, Burnham." Did Mom let go of my ear? Guess again. We marched down the street to the Central Illinois Light Company's office. Yes. People stopped to stare. This was becoming old hat for me by now, so I began to take the initiative and tell people that I had broken a street light. I didn't have time to tell them anything else because I was being whisked down the street at a rather rapid rate.

Up the stairs we went with great vigor to the main office. As we walked through the office doors the normally busy hubbub became a pregnant silence. All eyes were on Mom and me. My mom held this new audience in the palm of her other hand and made the final announcement of what I had done. She asked if she could speak to someone about the cost of replacing the street light I had broken. Mom didn't let go of my ear until we had the figure on paper and had set a time for me to pay this enormous bill with the money I would earn by mowing lawns and, yes, pulling weeds.

Throwing that rock at the street light has to be called a "wild pitch."

Two

THE MONEY PITCH

W hen I was about eleven years old, my dad decided to try something creative to help me out. He knew of a way that I could throw something and earn money instead of throwing something and paying money.

Dad bought two tickets for a Cardinal major league baseball game. I was excited as we headed for St. Louis. After watching the game for a while, Dad told me that these guys were paid big bucks for throwing, catching and hitting that baseball. I got the picture. I told Dad that these guys were older, bigger and stronger than I would ever be. He said, "You will get older." We laughed.

My dad pitched baseball when he was a teenager. He damaged his arm when he pitched twenty-one straight innings. No one told him that you could ruin your arm if you overdid it.

It had become painfully obvious to Dad that I liked to throw things. He thought that if I got interested in throwing a baseball it would benefit me and everyone else.

When a dad takes an interest in his son like this, good things begin to happen. At some point during the game I turned to Dad and told him I wanted to be a professional ball player someday.

Dad was happy to hear that. When we got home, Dad started to play catch with me and told me what and where the strike zone was. I practiced every chance I got. I would take my glove, a baseball and a catcher's mitt to our grade school playground, and a friend would catch while I pitched. In grade school, softball is normally the game to play. I played softball, but my heart was sold out to baseball.

As I was pitching to a friend at school one day, a big, well-dressed man in a business suit stood nearby watching. As I pitched to my friend, I pretended that this big guy was a baseball scout. You know how a kid can play games in his mind to motivate himself to do better? I was no exception. It wasn't long before this man came up to me and asked why I was throwing a baseball on a softball diamond. I told him I wanted to be a professional baseball pitcher someday so I thought I better get started practicing.

My friend came running up to see what we were talking about. Then this big guy showed us his right hand. It looked like every finger had been broken. When I asked him what had happened to his hand, he told us that he had been a catcher for the Boston Red Sox for thirteen years and that he was now a professional baseball scout. He told me to keep practicing and said that one day he might sign me to a professional baseball contract. He mentioned that I threw real good for a kid my age. He warned me not to throw any curve balls until I was a teenager.

Needless to say, I was on cloud nine. My buddy told me not to get my hopes up "because you are too skinny and too ugly to ever get your picture on a baseball card." I told him I wasn't too skinny, and he laughed. We both knew that there was a potential that I would gain weight, but I was stuck with my face. I had to develop my arm so I wouldn't worry about my face. The batter had to hit the ball, not my face, even though it looked like many people had hit my face at one time or another.

A guy who isn't handsome can at least develop a sense of humor. That's what I did. I love to laugh. I love to make others laugh just so I can laugh with them. The Bible says that laughter is like medicine to the soul. Because of that, some people have said that a person will live longer if he laughs a lot. Well, that's one reason I will probably live to be 120 years old. There is another reason I think I will live longer. I can just hear Moses saying to God: "No, Lord! Please, not yet. Don't bring Jon up here just yet. Remember, Lord, this is for eternity." It looks like I'll be down here for a good long time.

The motivation to pitch professionally stayed with me throughout my high school and college years. When I graduated from Woodruff High School in 1953, I got financial aid from Bradley University to play basketball and baseball. At that time Bradley had Leo Schrall, one of the top baseball coaches in the country. By the time I was a junior, I was a starter. We won the Missouri Valley Conference Championship that year in 1956. That same team went on to be inducted into the Greater Peoria Area Hall of Fame and the Bradley University Hall of Fame. Six of us signed professional baseball contracts.

Professional baseball scouts from every team in the major leagues came to this College World Series to pick, choose and, hopefully, sign some of these players to a contract with their club. This is where the Baltimore Oriole scout watched me pitch against the Big Ten champions, the University of Minnesota.

One inning I pitched to the first three batters, and they all reached first base. I was a right-handed pitcher. The Oriole scout was not impressed that all three reached first base, but he was impressed that I picked each one of them off first base. I guess the scout figured that if I couldn't get them out at home plate I would get them out at first. That became a one-inning record for a pitcher during a College World Series that could be tied but never broken.

The Minnesota team had a shortstop named Jerry Kendall who was to sign for a big bonus with the Cubs right after the College World Series was over. Another reason the Baltimore scout may have been interested in me was that I struck Jerry out three straight times. I found out later that he had earned the Big Ten Golden Glove award. One of the reasons they signed Jerry was for his ability to cover the shortstop position and not so much for his hitting ability, although he was a good hitter.

After graduating from Bradley in 1957, I signed with the Baltimore Orioles. Thanks, Dad. Thank you, too, Mom, for challenging me to pull all those weeds that gave strength to my hands and arms.

Dad's "money pitch" paid off.

Three

THE PREACHER'S PITCH

A t this point, signing with the Orioles was the most exciting moment of my life. I signed for a bonus that would give me and the girl I wanted to marry financial security that would last for at least two weeks. I asked Beverly Grant to marry me. When she accepted my proposal, that became the most exciting moment of my life.

I could now offer my bonus money as security to my fiancée's parents to show that I could provide for their daughter. Bev's dad and mom felt that I could fall back on my college diploma if baseball didn't work out, so they agreed to let me marry their daughter. All the excitement made me think that it just couldn't get any better than this. The plan was to marry Bev right after my first season of professional baseball with the Orioles.

The season had already begun when I joined the team in Aberdeen, South Dakota. I had a three-win and two-loss record when they shipped me to Paris, Texas, to finish up my first year.

Naturally, the guys in Texas had already picked their roommates before I arrived to join the team. The center fielder didn't have a roommate so he inherited me. I just figured that he didn't have a roommate because the numbers didn't work out.

I found out on the first night why he didn't have a roommate. He was going to be a preacher when his baseball career was over, and he had been practicing on his "former" roommates. No wonder the guys nicknamed me "Lucky" right off the bat. That first night "Preacher Boy" talked to me until 2:00 a.m. His leadoff question was: "Are you a Christian?" I said of course I was. He wanted to know why I thought I was a Christian. I told him that I was born in the United States. He laughed and asked me if I were born in a garage, would I be a car? I was insulted and figured he would never make it as a preacher. He had already lost the team as his first congregation, and now he seemed to be working on losing me. Besides, I figured if Preacher Boy didn't know that the United States was a Christian country, he had a lot to learn. I decided to humor him, so I stayed on as his roommate.

From time to time my little buddy, Preacher Boy, would try to convince me that he could help me if I ever got into trouble during a game I was pitching. He gave me an example of what he meant. He said: "If you have the bases loaded, say in the seventh inning, no one out and a three-no-count on the batter, just look out to center field, and I will shout instructions to you that will get you out of the inning." The very next game I was pitching, I realized it was the seventh inning and the bases were loaded; there was no one out, and I had a three-no-count on the batter. I realized then that my center fielder was not only a preacher; he was a prophet. I stepped off the mound to grab the rosin bag, and as I was rubbing the ball I just stood there looking out to center field. I figured that since Preacher Boy had set this whole thing up, he'd better keep his word and get me out of this inning. He saw me standing there looking out to center field. He threw his ball glove to the ground, cupped his hands around his mouth and yelled, "Burnham, Philippians 4:13!"

I looked out to the bull pen, and Philip wasn't even warming up. I murmured to myself, "Thanks a lot." I wound up and threw my next pitch. The batter hit a grand slam out of the ballpark. That was quite a "Preacher's Pitch." I decided then and there never to throw that pitch again.

He was a really good guy. With Preacher Boy as my roommate I still compiled a nine-win and three-loss record overall.

I'll never forget the "Preacher's Pitch."

Four

THE FAT PITCH

A t the end of the season the coach told me I would have to gain some weight before next spring training in order to have more endurance and power.

I was six-feet, five-inches tall but only weighed 170 pounds. I wasn't as intimidating as the coaches wanted me to be on the mound. They wanted me to stand out there on the mound and sneer at the hitter and say, "Me Bongo," and fire bullets.

I didn't scare anyone at the plate with my skinny frame. I did notice that when I would go into a stretch motion on the mound to hold a runner on first, the batter would step out of the batter's box with a funny look

21

on his face. When I turned sideways it looked, to the hitter, like I disappeared. Yes, I was very skinny. I had to run around in the shower to get wet.

I told the coaches not to worry about me gaining weight. I had a game plan. When I got home I was going to get married. I noticed that when any of my buddies got married they gained weight. I thought I would try it.

I had added incentive. During the winter negotiations I was given a Double A contract but was to join our Triple A ball club for spring training. This was quite a jump from the lower minors.

If I made the Triple A team, I would only be one step from the big leagues.

I took to heart what the coaches said about gaining weight. I wanted to marry Bev not only because I loved her but because she was a great cook as well. We got married September 21, 1957, and I gained fifty pounds before the next spring training. Was I right or what?

I rolled into spring training camp and had to introduce myself to the coaches. They didn't recognize me. They told me that I had overdone it and that I would have to run off the excess weight. The extra weight threw off my delivery, especially the curve ball. The coaches noticed how accurate I had become, hitting the bat with almost every pitch. It was truly impressive. The coaches got their heads together and were remarking about it with awe and great wonder. I kept hearing the disparaging cry of the "Oh, No" bird. "Oh, no! Oh, no! Oh, no!"

Things only got worse. My attitude hit an all-time low. The Triple A club dropped me to a Class A team in Georgia to finish my spring training. After working out with the Triple A club on the soft turf of Florida, I was moved to the hard clay of Georgia. I developed painful shin splints. The pain threw my pitching delivery off even more. I developed a sore arm that felt like it was dangling from the socket. It was at this point that Bev told me she really didn't like baseball, especially since the batters were consistently hitting line drives off her husband's body. She liked watching me pitch, but at this point it was not a pretty sight.

It was time to go back home to Peoria. The Oriole organization had me sign a retirement contract so that no other club could sign me if I changed my mind during the next two years.

The "fat pitch" really did me in. Bev's cooking made me fat, but we also found out what kind of "taste" she had for baseball.

Five

THE FUNNY PITCH

B ev and I drove back to Peoria, Illinois, to begin life without baseball. I felt like a total failure. I wanted to hide in the small apartment we rented. I didn't want to run into anybody who had expected me to make it big in baseball. Pride made me think the whole world noticed.

As I was watching TV one evening, Ed Sullivan came on with his "Really Big Shuuu." He was introducing Don Adams, a bright, young, new comedian. You remember Don Adams. He went on to have his own TV series, *Get Smart*.

I was ready for a good laugh even though I felt like I would never laugh again. When I saw the skit Don performed, I literally rolled on the floor with laughter. All of a sudden I realized that right there before my eyes was the humorous way to explain why I didn't make it in professional baseball.

You see, Don Adams did his skit about umpires. He made umpires look terrible. Umpires progress through the minors just like ball players do in order to become major league umpires. Now I could claim that the umpires were so bad that they never gave me the corners when I pitched. That would explain my lack of success in the minor leagues.

Do you want to know how the skit went? Sure you do, so here goes...

Don came on stage with a baseball cap, clipboard and a whistle tied around his neck. He instructed the audience to go along with him as he was going to portray himself to be the coach of an umpire school. The audience was to pretend that they were there to become the future umpires of America.

Got the picture? Good. Here's the skit:

Don, speaking: "Men! So you want to become umpires? Alright. It's going to be a long tough row to hoe for each and every one of you. Some of you will succeed, and others will crack. For those of you who succeed, you will go on to bigger and better things. For those of you who crack, you will become umpires.

"Monday morning I want you here promptly at 7:00 a.m. sharp. We will begin our rigorous training program with plate dusting and bottle dodging.

"Tuesday...Graduation!

"If you can answer this final examination quiz, you will pass with flying colors. There is a man on first and a man on third."

Don stopped all of a sudden and looked into the audience, as if he had spotted someone, and said:

"Let me stop the quiz right here. Schmidly and

Jonesy, you have been coming to this camp for the last five years. Now, it is true that a first base umpire and a third base umpire go hand in hand, but not on the field, men!

"Now, on with the quiz. There is a man on first and a man on third. It's the seventh inning with no one out. The batter hits a long fly ball to the center fielder. The center fielder loses the ball in the sun, and it hits him on the head and falls harmlessly to the ground. An irritated fan throws a hand grenade into the bull pen killing seven bulls. An ice cream vendor runs onto the field and tries to proposition the shortstop. The man on first goes to third. That man on third goes to first. What is your decision? Chocolate or vanilla?"

Well, maybe you had to be there to see what I saw, hear what I heard and feel like I felt to appreciate the skit as much as I did. I got a lot of mileage out of that skit over the years, blaming the minor league umpires for my demise.

Don delivered a truly "funny pitch."

Six

THE CLEAN-UP PITCH

Bev's dad was concerned that I didn't make it in baseball. He was more concerned when I told him that I wasn't cut out to be a teacher or a coach. To make a long story short, Bev's dad wanted to make sure his daughter had clothes on her back and food on the table, so he offered me a job in the dry cleaning business that he and his partner had owned and operated for thirty years.

I thought that I, being a college graduate, could certainly learn this business. I rather enjoyed watching the clothes tumble around and shrink. This was not difficult at all. The customers gave me many opportunities to learn diplomacy and how to dodge bullets.

Dad and his partner had a policy not to hire family on a permanent basis. What Bev's dad decided to do was just great. He heard that a cleaning plant in Morton, Illinois, was up for sale. It was a small one-horse plant. He figured that by using his own business expertise he could purchase this business and let me run it for a salary. In the fall of 1958 Dad bought the business. Peoria wasn't far from Morton so he could run over and help me when a machine broke down or help me ease the agony of a dissatisfied customer. I was such an egotist that I thought since I had been a pro-baseball player from nearby Peoria, the people from Morton would be thrilled to bring their dry cleaning to "Me."

Why was I so sure? During my athletic years with Woodruff High, Bradley University and the Orioles, I would save the clippings from the sports page of the Peoria paper, especially if my name was in the headlines. I put two and two together and knew that most of the residents in Morton got the Peoria paper. How could they not see my name? I thought the people in Morton would be happy to have me in their town cleaning their clothes. Guess again, Burnham.

After being in business for just a short time, I found that they didn't care who I was, who I "thought" I was or where I came from. Let me explain. I remember a little lady who came in to pick up her husband's trousers. She had already heard about the quality of work we did, so she took the trousers out of the bag to look at them before leaving for home. She felt she might as well save herself a trip back to our plant if she found a flaw in our workmanship before she left.

She held the trousers up to look at them and said in a perfectly sarcastic tone, "I'm not impressed with these accordion pleats running down the right leg of my husband's pants!"

I replied in a perfectly sarcastic tone, "Well, pick one of those creases out, lady, and I'll sharpen it up."

Is it any wonder that the people of Morton doubted that I would survive in business for even one year? Bev's dad and I had become real close. We went hunting and fishing together. I admired how he could run a business and raise a son like Larry and a daughter like Bev. He built his own home, flew his own airplane and did his own income tax return. He was quite a guy. I really hung on to his coattails.

Six weeks after we were in business, Bev's dad died in a freak accident while changing the oil in his car. It was a windy day, and the car jack was not stable enough. The car fell on him, and he died instantly. Bev was so close to her dad, and I felt terrible for her sake. Not only did she lose her dad, but she was about to give birth to our first son, Lee, and she had been looking forward to having her dad there to influence Lee.

Bev and I say "thanks" to her dad for getting us into a business that God used to help change our lives. It was a great "clean-up pitch!" Bev and I would use this pitch for the next twenty years.

Seven

THE COME ON PITCH

My attitude got worse right away because I didn't have Bev's dad to lean on. My "locker room lingo" came blasting out when a machine would break down, when employees would quit and when customers complained. It was pretty discouraging for the housewives who were working for me to put up with an egotistical, foul-mouthed punk like me.

After two years of this hell on earth, I noticed that Bev had lost the gleam in her eye for me. I asked her what was wrong with me, and she said she didn't know.

During those rotten years I tried using what I learned in sports. I felt all I had to do was to bull my neck and hang in there. My bull neck didn't seem to work in this tough game of real life.

About that time a businessman by the name of Harold "Hap" Edwards dropped in to the cleaning plant to invite me to go to a Christian Businessmen's committee meeting that met once a month. I had the Preacher Boy roommate in baseball, and now here was another guy asking me to go to some religious meeting. Mr. Edwards kept coming back, and I kept turning him down even though he said he would pay my way. Each time he came back, I noticed he never acted offended when I turned him down.

One time, right after Hap came in with another invitation, a neighbor of ours, Maurice Stahly, asked me and my wife to go with him and his wife to that same meeting. Maurice couldn't help but see how I acted around the house and neighborhood. He knew for sure that I was not a happy camper.

It looked to me like Maurice and Hap had a game plan to reach me, this foul-mouthed kid who was trying to run a business and raise a family. I know now that God was the one trying to get my attention, and He was using two different men and all kinds of situations to get the job done. I wanted to be neighborly, plus wives usually like to eat out, so I said yes.

The "come-on pitch" finally got to me. I thank God for the men He used to finally get me to that meeting.

Eight

THE WINNING PITCH

The evening came to go to the banquet with Maurice and Opal. When we got there, Bev and I were ushered into the basement of a big church in Washington, Illinois. Many people were sitting there talking and waiting to be served the meal. Our seats just happened to be very close to the head table. At the head table sat the speaker, the chairman and his wife, the master of ceremonies, the song leader, and the soloist.

I was eating away trying to make small talk with my mouth half open and full of food. My wife gave me some undigested glances from time to time, but my glance back reminded her that I was only here for the meal.

The song leader got up and wanted everyone to start singing. I wasn't done with my dessert, plus I wanted to finish off what Bev had left. The group could get along without me singing. I continued to feed my face.

The songs they were singing were hymns. This was beginning to sound like a church service. That didn't really bother me all that much. I had been to church before. Church, after all, had been a great place to look over the crop of good-looking gals that might be available.

They were into their third song when some lady came along and took my plate away. This was a huge hint to stop eating. The fun was over, and the time to endure the rest of the evening was upon me.

The master of ceremonies got up and introduced a man who told a story about how a fellow soldier helped save his life on the battlefield. He made a promise that if he ever got out of the war alive he would give his life to God and try to be as diligent as two men for the sake of his buddy who had died to save this man's life. I was impressed.

The soloist sang a few songs. I noticed that no one was smoking and talking while she sang. This was really a genuine evening. I wondered what the main speaker was going to say. The guy who spoke before was cool, and I was getting into this. The chairman of the meeting stood to introduce the speaker:

"Ladies and gentlemen, we are privileged to present to you this evening a man who is a retired general from the United States Army. This was one of the men who signed the Second World War Peace Treaty. Let's welcome General William Harrison."

The place quieted down after a round of applause. General Harrison was not a very tall man, but he stood there with authority.

He looked slowly around the room with a smile

on his face. He took his time and seemed to look into the eyes of everyone there before he said a word. Finally, I poked my wife in the ribs and said, "This guy's weird. Look at him staring at us like that."

Then General Harrison spoke. "Did you know that God loves you and has a wonderful plan for your life?"

I didn't know it at the time, but he was on the board of Campus Crusade for Christ International. He began to present the gospel in a very clear and understandable way. He continued:

"Just as there are physical laws that govern the physical universe, so there are spiritual laws that govern our relationship with God. If I stand here and drop a pencil, it will always fall on the floor due to the physical law of gravity. If a person jumps off a twenty-story building, he will fall due to that same law of gravity, and he's likely to die when he hits the ground. These spiritual laws are just as consistent and just as profound as God's physical laws.

"The first law is that God loves you and has a wonderful plan for your life. Are you experiencing that plan?"

The General quoted John 3:16: "For God so loved the world, that He gave his only begotten Son, that whosoever believeth in Him should not perish, but have everlasting life."

I had heard that verse before. Then he looked into the audience and said, "God included everyone in this room when He spoke about loving the world. He brought it down to one person when He said, 'whosoever.'

"In John 3:16 God only mentioned the whosoever who believes and said that he will go to heaven. That left room for the other whosoever—the whosoever who doesn't believe. The whosoever who doesn't believe will go to hell."

34

Hold the phone. That got my attention. He said the word hell. I figured this guy was alright. Now he's talking my language.

Then he really got my attention when he said, "Which whosoever are you? If you believe in Christ, you're going to heaven. If you don't believe in Him, you'll go to hell. Believe means to commit your life to Him."

I was beginning to see how he got to be a general in the army. He shot from the hip. He didn't mess around, and I liked that. He was a real man's man.

I was hoping that I was one of the good guys. I had tried to convince Preacher Boy that I was one of the good guys.

He quoted from John 10:10b: "I am come that they might have life, and that they might have it more abundantly." Then he asked, "Are you experiencing a rich, meaningful life?"

I was sure I wasn't. He said, "Do you know why most people are not experiencing the abundant life? The answer is found in law two.

"The second law indicates that man is sinful and separated from God, and thus he cannot know and experience God's love and plan for his life."

When the General mentioned being sinful, I started getting upset inside. It doesn't take a mental giant to figure out what sin is. I had quite a foul mouth, told dirty jokes and my thought life left much to be desired. This got me thinking of a lot of stupid things I had done. His comment about being a sinner started all this junk racing through my mind and my face started getting red.

During the years I went to school, there would be times when I would be embarrassed in class for one reason or another. When that happened, my face would get red. At those times there always seemed to be someone behind me who would say, "Look at Burnham's face get red."

Now here I was at this banquet with my wife, minding my own business, and all of a sudden my face is getting red for all to see. I didn't know the people behind me, but I thought for sure I heard someone say: "Look at that guy's face get red." Hearing that, my head pounded with every heartbeat—boom, boom, boom. My face must have looked like a flashing neon sign. I felt like I opened the door for the General to point at me and say, "Now here we have a prime example of a sinner. I don't know what your problem is, young man, but it must be a doozy."

Even though he didn't say a word about me, I was ticked at him for triggering my mind to do this instant review of my tarnished mental memory bank. Now I was paying the price publicly with my red face.

General Harrison went on to explain: "Since man is sinful he will try most anything to fill the void in his life. He'll try a variety of things like philosophy, good life, ethics and so on, to fill that void. He will always fall short of the peace of mind he's looking for."

General Harrison quoted another Scripture verse— Romans 3:23: "For *all* have sinned, and come short of the glory of God."

He said, "Let me break that verse down."

I had never heard anyone break a verse down before. I thought, "This ought to be good."

He said, "The word *all* covers a lot of ground. That means your mom, dad, husband, wife, sisters, brothers, aunts, uncles, Sunday school teachers, ministers, priests, rabbis and even the librarian."

Wow, who would have thought?

I poked my wife in the ribs and said, "That means you too." Wouldn't you know it, her face got red. Now I felt like I wasn't all alone, and I began to like the

General again.

Then he dropped another bomb. He quoted another verse, Romans 6:23: "For the wages of sin is death..." (a spiritual separation from God).

He said, "Man was created to have fellowship with God, but because of his own stubborn self-will, man chose to go his own independent way, and fellowship was broken. If you die in that condition, you will go to hell."

Now I was down in the mouth again because I knew these verses were talking about me. My mind went into fast forward. I thought if I didn't die I would have it made. The problem is that everyone dies someday. This is something I couldn't control, and I began to feel helpless.

"The third law gives us the only answer to this dilemma. Law three tells us that Jesus Christ is God's only provision for man's sin. Through Him you can know God's love and plan for your life."

The General quoted another verse, Romans 5:8: "But God commendeth His love for us, in that, while we were yet sinners, Christ died for us." Then he quoted John 14:6: "Jesus said unto him, 'I am the way, the truth, and the life: no man cometh unto the Father, but by me.'"

The General said, "There is a gap between sinful man and Holy God. Man cannot bridge that gap by his own efforts. So what did God do? He sent His Son, Jesus Christ, to bridge that gap by dying on the cross to wash away our sins. Jesus made it possible for us to get to God and the abundant life."

General Harrison pointed out that it wasn't enough to know these three laws or even to believe them. He told us that the fourth law gives us the opportunity to do something about it. He said, "The fourth law indicates that we must receive Jesus Christ as Savior and Lord by personal invitation."

He said, "Let me explain what Savior and Lord means. *Savior* means He will save you from hell and save you for heaven. *Lord* means He will save you from you. *Lord* means boss.

Coaches had told me that I was my own worst enemy. To have a Lord that would save me from me was what I needed. I saw what had happened to me when I was boss.

He quoted John 1:12: "But as many as received him, to them gave he power to become the sons of God, even to them that believe on His name."

I remember him saying, "To believe is to commit your life to Christ. After all, who could run your life better than the one who created you?"

The General stopped and looked around the room. "Listen closely," He said "This next verse is very personal. The Bible says in Revelation 3:20, 'Behold, I stand at the door, and knock: if any man hear my voice, and open the door, I will come in to him...' "

It was at this point that I really felt empty inside. I didn't hear any voices, so I thought I just wasn't spiritual enough to become a Christian. I must be too callous.

The General said, "Let me break that verse down."

I had liked the way he broke down Romans 3:23. He put us all in the same boat with that verse, including my wife. Now he said, "Any time you hear what Jesus was quoted to have said, you've heard Him say it. Tonight you've heard my voice quoting what Jesus said. In essence, you heard Jesus say it. What did He say? He is standing and knocking at the door of your heart and life right now. He wants to come in. The choice is yours."

What really nailed it down for me was when General Harrison quoted 1 John 5:10-13: "He that believeth on the Son of God hath the witness in himself: he that believeth not God hath made Him a liar; because he believeth not the record that God gave of his Son. And this is the record, that God hath given to us eternal life, and this life is in his Son. He that *has* the Son *has* life (right now); and he that *has not* the Son of God *has not* life. These things have I written unto you that believe on the name of the Son of God; that ye may *know* that ye *have* eternal life"(caps and parentheses added).

Now you have seen the "winning pitch."

What have you done with that pitch? God used General Harrison to throw the "winning pitch" in my life and I hope in yours as well.

I received Jesus Christ as my Savior and Lord that night — October 9, 1961.

Nine

THE CURVE BALL PITCH

The next day at work I was inspecting a pair of trousers. By accident I dropped them on the dusty floor. I got ticked and swore, using the Lord's name in vain. I swore just like I used to when I would lose a ball game. Now I was upset about swearing right after receiving Jesus Christ as my Savior and Lord the night before. Why was I still swearing? Wasn't I supposed to be changed? I thought if Christ really came into my life I wouldn't be swearing anymore. I had tried to stop this bad habit before I received Jesus Christ into my life. I had not been successful.

I was angry enough to challenge God right on the spot. In my mind I sent up a screaming prayer. If I had yelled that prayer out loud the employees would have walked off the job for sure. In my mind I yelled, "If You really came into my life last night, let me see You clean up my mouth. You created everything—trees, plants and animals—and You hold the universe together. You can surely clean up my mouth!"

After praying with such belligerence, I didn't know what to expect. For all I knew God might have come down through the ceiling with a bolt of lightning, so I quickly stepped aside. Talk about being conceited. Just to think that I could step aside fast enough to avoid God zapping me must have made Him laugh. Obviously the Lord didn't zap me. Instead, He threw me a "curve ball." Why am I calling it a "curve ball"? It was God's way to help me overcome my swearing.

Since He did something different than what I thought He would do, I refer to what He did as throwing me a "curve ball." We can't figure God out with human reasoning. He enjoys proving Himself to us in a most loving and creative way.

Here is the "curve ball." I went over to the steam press to finish pressing some sports coats. As I pulled the press head down, I noticed a flat area on the top of it that had never been significant to me before. I also got a thought I never had before: "Put some Scripture cards on the top of your press head." To me that seemed to be the craziest thought I had ever had, so I simply dismissed it from my mind. The next day I had the very same thought. This time I muttered under my breath: "I don't have any Scripture cards, and I'm not going to tear a page out of the Bible either. Where are these weird thoughts coming from anyway?"

An employee working at a press next to mine asked, "What did you say, Jon?"

In my mind I said to myself, "Oh, no! Now my employees will think I'm a religious fanatic talking to myself like this." About this time the mailman came in the front door with some mail. I went up to see if there was something for me. Sure enough, there was an envelope with my name on it. I opened it, and four Navigator Scripture cards fell out on my desk. I couldn't believe my eyes. I never knew there were such things as Scripture cards. I had thoughts about Scripture cards, and here they were. What was I going to do with these cards? If the employees saw me put those cards on the top of my press head, they would believe I really was a religious fanatic.

I waited until everyone had gone home for the day before I pulled those Scripture cards out of my pocket. I pulled the press head down and taped the cards on the flat area of the press head. When I let go, the press head sprang back up, and the cards were out of sight.

From then on, as I worked at that press, I would pull the press head down and memorize those verses. When someone would come up to talk with me, I would simply let go of the press head, and the cards would spring up out of sight.

Talk about a chicken Christian. This chicken program went on for a few months until Yvonne, my twin sister, came into the plant to see me. I let go of the press head. The cards disappeared from sight. At that very moment the Lord put this convicting thought in my mind: "You played guts basketball, you played guts baseball, you chicken Christian!"

In immediate response to that thought I pulled the press head down with great vigor, allowing my sister to see the Scripture cards. Yvonne looked at them and said: "Aw, Jonny's gone religious!"

I looked at her and asked, "Yvonne, where are you going when you die?" Not *if* you die, *when* you die. My sister had no answer.

At that point in my young Christian life I didn't

know how to explain salvation to her. Looking back now I realize God's timing was perfect. My sister wasn't ready for that pitch. Besides, I hadn't learned enough about the "winning pitch" to throw it to her.

Let's go back to God's "curve ball." A year and a half after I screamed out that belligerent prayer to God, I realized I wasn't swearing anymore. I had fully expected Him to zap me, but instead He gave me the desire to memorize those Scriptures. That was His perfectly thrown "curve ball." He didn't scream at me each time I swore during those next few months.

Instead, His Word changed the way I thought. His Word reprogrammed my mind. His way of changing me was far different from what I thought He would do to clean up my mouth. He threw me a "curve ball." I mentioned this to Bev and found that she had already noticed the change in me. She said that even my attitude was better.

When we think we know how God will deal with us, we may very well see Him pitch a "curve ball" instead. We might even find ourselves saying, "Wow, let me see that pitch again."

Ten

THE MEDICINE PITCH

I wanted to learn how to throw the "winning pitch." I also wanted to have a good curve ball of my own. Being a competitive, egotistical baseball pitcher, I wanted to help God get others into His kingdom. I wanted to learn how to set up the batter, as it were, to strike him out so he would see the need to come to Christ for salvation. I pictured this as a spiritual game to win just like those baseball games I used to play.

I was too young of a Christian to know that God didn't need my help. In a later chapter, I will tell you how He made that point very clear with another one of His unique "curve balls." How wonderful and kind He is to have such patience with us.

I bought a book by Dr. Walter Wilson entitled *Miracles of a Doctor.* This Christian doctor told many stories about how he saw God change secular conversations into spiritual ones. Dr. Wilson would then lead those people to Christ. He was a godly man.

As I read his book I noticed that he loved Jesus and prayed consistently for guidance. He prayed that he would be led to people whom the Lord was making ready to receive the "Winning Pitch."

One story was about a friend who gave Dr. Wilson the address of a man named Charlie Johnson. Dr. Wilson was to visit that town soon, so he went to visit Mr. Johnson. He knocked at the door, and a young woman answered. He told her he was looking for Mr. Johnson, and she invited him in.

During a short conversation, it became evident that this was not the residence of the Mr. Johnson he was seeking.

Dr. Wilson had prayed prior to coming to this address that the Lord would guide him. He knew the Lord doesn't make mistakes so He must have a reason for this situation. He had noticed as he came into the living room that there were two people sitting at a table upon which lay an open Bible. Dr. Wilson reasoned that they must have been having a Bible study.

As he was leaving, he cried out to God for he felt the visit was planned of God. Many thoughts were going through his mind as he was getting ready to leave. Approaching the center of the room, he picked up the Bible from the table and inquired, "Do you read this book, Mrs. Johnson, and do you love it?"

At once all three of them looked at each other with astonishment, as though their minds were stirred to ask some questions. "Yes," Mrs. Johnson answered quickly and firmly. "We love that book in this home."

Dr. Wilson then asked, "Have you found out from

its pages how you may be saved and know it?"

By this time the hearts of these three were so stirred that they could not restrain the tears. They looked at each other in such a peculiar way that he sensed immediately that some strange thing was transpiring. After Mrs. Johnson regained control of her feelings, she asked, "Dr. Wilson, do you understand that Bible? Can you tell us how we may be saved?"

Dr. Wilson said, "Yes, indeed, that is my principle business in life. I would be glad to help you understand."

Mrs. Johnson told him how they had just been praying that the Lord would send someone who could tell them how they could know the way to have eternal life. Needless to say, Dr. Wilson led all three of those people to a saving knowledge of Jesus Christ.

It became my desire that I would pray like Dr. Wilson did so that I would be sensitive to the Holy Spirit's direction as to what to say. I had a long way to go. The next story gave me confidence that the Lord will work in spite of us.

In this next story Dr. Wilson showed his human side by not being as sensitive as he knew he could be. This story encouraged me because insensitivity seemed to be my middle name.

Dr. Wilson told a story about a woman who worked for him in his tent factory. Being a doctor, he took care of any employees who might get injured on the job. One day Bertha, a female employee, came in with an injury to her finger. Dr. Wilson fixed it and told her that her sewing machine had been checked and was in good working order and to be more careful.

About ten days later the same young lady came in again with a more severe injury to her finger. He took care of it and told her that the machine was checked again and that she was simply being careless. He said, "If you are injured once more, I will have to advise the foreman to dismiss you."

Another ten days passed when, to Dr. Wilson's astonishment, Bertha presented herself a third time. She was overcome with pain. This time the needle was driven into the bone of her finger and had broken off inside the bone. This called for Dr. Wilson's surgical skills to treat this injury.

After Dr. Wilson removed the needle and dressed the wound, he looked at Bertha quite earnestly and said, "I am sorry, Bertha, but I'm going to have to let you go. The Scriptures say, 'Thou knowest not what a day may bring forth.' This is a serious accident. You may suffer from blood poisoning. You don't know what complications may follow. Are you ready to meet God? Have you arranged with the Lord for your trip to eternity? Tell me, Bertha, has this ever been considered by you seriously?"

She leaned on the table, looked him in the eye and said, "Doctor, you have asked me a question that has troubled me greatly for some weeks. I am not ready to die. I do not have peace with God, and this is the third time I have come to your office in order that you might tell me how to be saved. I was not careless at the machine, and I know there is nothing wrong with the machine.

"I deliberately placed my finger under the needle the first time thinking that while you were dressing it you would talk to me about Jesus. I went away from your desk disappointed. I felt you didn't care about my soul.

"I did the same thing again, hoping this time you would tell me, and again you let me leave your office with no help for my heart. I was so disappointed and heartbroken to think that you would not help me to be saved that I have cried most of the time since then and have not been able to eat nor sleep as I should.

"This morning," she continued, "I came to work with the determination to injure myself so severely that you would have to give me more time and perhaps would think of my soul. I deliberately put my finger under that needle. I was willing to suffer the pain and run the risk of losing my hand if only you would talk with me about the salvation of my soul."

Dr. Wilson felt terrible because he had been out of touch with the Lord the first two days Bertha had come. Then Dr. Wilson promptly led Bertha to Christ, and she said it was worth all the pain.

His testimony of talking to people about Jesus had evidently preceded him. Bertha must have heard that Dr. Wilson would tell anyone and everyone about his Savior.

From this I learned that I must stay close to the Lord so I won't miss an opportunity to tell others about Jesus.

Yes, the big lie is that people don't really care about spiritual things. I thank God for His timing in my life by encouraging me to read about how He used Dr. Walter Wilson in everyday life. The doctor prayed, and God set the stage for him to meet many people in need of the Savior.

The Lord gave Dr. Walter Wilson a great "medicine pitch."

I found that you don't have to be a doctor to use that pitch. Why? The Lord Himself is the Great Physician. He gives us the medicine to give to others. In fact, He is the medicine that gives a person eternal life if and when that person chooses to take the medicine.

Dr. Walter Wilson was faithful to dispense the medicine.

The "medicine pitch" can change a person from death to life. It is my prayer that you have taken this wonderful medicine—Jesus Christ—as your Savior and Lord.

Eleven

THE MEMORY PITCH

The desire to witness to people really got to me, showing me that Jesus still teaches people how to become "fishers of men." I loved fishing, but in this case I knew very little along this *line*. No pun intended.

It wasn't long after I got this desire from God, after reading Dr. Wilson's book, that I heard of a Christian organization that taught Christian people how to share their faith. There was a meeting scheduled in a small town many miles away from my home for people interested in learning how to share about their faith in Jesus. My wife and I were both interested so we didn't hesitate to go.

The leader of the meeting introduced a local farmer who told a story that impressed us a great deal. The farmer's story follows:

"I got up one morning thinking about a hired hand of mine who had some problems. I left instructions for him to plow a field that was about a mile from my farm house.

"As I was eating breakfast I was convicted about not having told him about Jesus, my personal problem solver. As soon as I finished eating, I pulled on my boots and went out the back door to start my long walk out to the field I told him to plow. I felt today was the day.

"He saw me coming a long way off and headed the tractor in my direction. As I approached, he turned the tractor off. We just talked small talk for a while, and then I asked him how things were going in his life. He saw I was concerned enough about his life to walk all the way out there, so he opened up and told me of one problem after another.

"I was all ready to encourage him about how he could have all the help he needed by trusting Jesus Christ, but before I said a word I reached into my shirt pocket for a pamphlet that I learned to use in leading people to Christ. I discovered that in my haste to leave the house I had forgotten to bring the pamphlet with me. I told him to go ahead and plow while I went back to the house to get something. I felt like kicking myself for not having the tract with me. He seemed to be so ready to hear the gospel, but without the tract I didn't feel confident enough to tell him about Jesus.

"I took off walking as fast as I could over those clods back to the house to get that tract. It seemed like it took me forever to get back home. I ran in the house and grabbed the tract and started out again toward the field.

"I had only walked a hundred yards when a cloudburst seemed to come out of nowhere. I ran for cover. I waited for the rain to stop, but it kept pouring. I figured my hired hand would simply get off the tractor and get in his pickup truck and go home.

"I figured I would have another chance to talk to him in a few days. I didn't. He killed himself that night. Talk about feeling sick inside.

"I know God's timing is perfect. I didn't know for sure if this man was a Christian or not. I wanted to make sure by sharing the gospel with him. God knows where that man is today.

"God used that incident in my life to impress upon me the need to use the brains He gave me to memorize a way to explain salvation so that I wouldn't be so dependent on a tract. A tract is a very good tool, and I recommend using them, but don't depend on them so much that you can't lead someone to Christ without it. After all, this message should come from our heart. If you have the tract memorized, the person you are sharing with will see and hear that this whole thing is really part of your life."

That was the end of the farmer's story, but it was the beginning of many of my own stories. God used his story to motivate me to do something I never thought I would. What's that? To exercise my brain to memorize many Scriptures that would make salvation clear enough for even a person with half a mind.

I thank God for that Christian farmer. He went on to tell other stories about how memorizing the way of salvation from the Scriptures increased his opportunities to share his faith. When the Lord sees you mean business like this, He will bring people to you.

The Lord honored that Christian farmer's "memory pitch."

Have you used your mind to memorize from the Scriptures a way to tell others about Jesus?

Twelve

THE HUMBLE PITCH

Here I was, ready, willing and able to witness. I had the desire to witness. I had the Scriptures memorized that explained salvation as clear as a bell. To my surprise I wasn't leading anyone to Christ. I thought, *What's the deal? Others are having success doing this. What's the matter with me?*

I had been going to church regularly. I was giving my tithe to God. I was praying and reading the Bible to my wife. I was having devotions with my family. I was an honest businessman. What more could God want from a guy? I was eager to play this "witnessing" game and win some souls for God.

During a Wednesday evening church service I was

sitting there listening to our pastor, Dr. Bruce Dunn, explain a situation he experienced a few weeks before. I didn't expect God to give me an answer to my dilemma from what Dr. Dunn was talking about, but He did. The following is what Dr. Dunn was sharing that night:

"As you know, we are in the process of choosing elders. A man who has been in this church for years came up to me and asked, 'Am I not elder material?'

"I said, 'No.'"

As I listened to these comments from the pastor, I was getting a different message from my Lord. I was too young to even think about being an elder, but I had been asking God, "Am I not witness material?" It was as though God said, "No."

As Dr. Dunn went on, God continued His thought process to me.

"Jon, you played baseball and basketball. As a baseball pitcher you got the ball back after every pitch so the game could continue. You felt that you were the center of attention. In basketball you were the tallest guy on the team, and you loved it when you were the high point man. You even got a few headlines on the sports page.

"The problem is that you became an egotist. Now you want to play this game of witnessing to win some souls for Me. Jon, I really don't need your help. In your present state of mind you are not witness material. Jon, this is not a 'game.' This is a matter of life or death. This is a matter of heaven or hell. I'm going to have to teach you how to step aside and let Me do what only I can do. I save a person's soul. I give them new life.

"You are experiencing the joy of a new life that I gave you, and you want others to have it too. That's good, but I have noticed that you have the mindset of a former jock. Your human view of things will have to change, and I will help you do that."

55

About the time my Lord got his point across to my mind, the pastor was wrapping up his message for the evening. I thank God for both Dr. Dunn's message and the message my Lord gave me.

I thank God for His "humble pitch" to me. It reminded me of the "curve ball" He had thrown me earlier. Both pitches were impressive. I didn't know it at the time, but He was about to show me how to throw an "eighteen-inch pitch."

Thirteen

THE EIGHTEEN-INCH PITCH

E arly the next morning I was in the back of the cleaning plant watching the clothes in the dryer tumble around and shrink. Lynda, our high school counter girl, came in to wait on customers before she went to school. I had the desire to witness to her, but I remembered what I had learned the night before. The Lord was going to teach me how to step aside and let Him do what only He can do.

All of a sudden my heart started pounding, my hands turned clammy and my tongue turned to cotton. I asked the Lord what was happening. I had no affection for this girl. I was a happily married man. This must be the natural nervousness that takes place when God is involved in a witnessing experience. Before, when I was on my own, I wasn't this nervous. I just went out and nailed people. I felt I had a job to do for God. I was now experiencing what it was like to lay back and depend on Him. He reminded me that this is a heaven or hell situation and that I should let Him lead. I was so humbled the night before that I told God that He would have to give me the words to say. I was determined not to witness on my own anymore.

A few customers had come in so I went up to get the clothes that Lynda tagged in for cleaning. As I was walking back with the clothes, Lynda was hovering over the sewing machine mending something. I said, "Hi, Lynda. Do you know how far it is between heaven and hell?"

She kept her head down and said, "No, I don't, Jon."

I said, "OK," and shot back to the back room with my heart pounding like crazy. I asked God, "Did You hear what I just said? She won't want to come back to work. She must think I'm crazy."

The Lord's thought came to me: *"I know what you said. Who do you think told you to say that? Jon, I know what I'm doing."* I was sure He did, and I was committed to go through with this and learn how to step aside.

The next morning, to my surprise, Lynda came in to work. I told the Lord that I was determined to let Him lead. I wasn't going to say a word, especially after what I said the morning before. If He was in this witnessing experience, He would have to show me. I went up front to get the clothes Lynda had tagged in for cleaning. As I went by, I saw her hovering over the sewing machine, obviously hiding from me. I got the tagged clothes, and as I was walking back she said, "Jon, how far is it between heaven and hell?"

I was so surprised that God prompted her to ask that I forgot everything I had memorized. I said, "Uh, uh, I'll bring my New Testament tomorrow and show you." I then shot back to the back room. My arm pits were dripping wet, my tongue turned to cotton and my palms were wet. I said, "Lord, I'm a mess. I'm going to have to go home and change shirts."

The next morning I had my New Testament with me, and you can imagine how nervous I was. Again I purposed not to bring up our conversation the morning before. Lynda came in and had waited on some customers. I went to the front to get the clothes she tagged for cleaning. As I was heading to the back Lynda said, "Jon, did you bring your New Testament to show me how far it is between heaven and hell?"

What was also interesting to me about that morning was that the fog was so thick that Irene's husband was concerned enough to drive her to work early. Irene was not only one of our clothes finishers, but she could wait on customers as well. With Irene there, I was able to share with Lynda without being interrupted by customers.

I took my New Testament from my pocket and began to show Lynda the distance between heaven and hell. Talk about God's timing and God's fog! We have never had fog like that before that would cause Irene to come to work early.

"Do you know the distance between heaven and hell?" Lynda already knew about Jesus in her mind. That's called head knowledge. That morning Lynda received Jesus Christ into her heart. The normal distance between the head and the heart is about *eighteen inches*. She knew who Jesus was but had never personally trusted that He died for *her* sins.

I have talked to many people who thought they were Christians because they knew many facts about

Christianity in their minds. Until we take these facts into our heart and believe by faith that they belong to us personally, we remain *eighteen inches* from heaven.

What are these facts? Jesus loves us and has a wonderful plan for our lives (John 3:16). We are sinful and separated from God, so how could we know His plan for us (Rom. 3:23)? Jesus Christ is God's provision for us in that He alone is the way to heaven (John 14:6). We must receive Him as personal Savior and Lord (John 1:12).

"He that believth in the Son of God hath the witness in himself: he that believeth not God hath made him a liar; because he believeth not the record that God gave of his Son. And this is the record, that God has *given* to us eternal life, and this life is in his Son. He that *has* the Son *has* life (right now); and he that has not the Son of God has not life. These things have I written unto you that believe on the name of the Son of God; that ye may *know* that ye *have* eternal life" (1 John 5:10-13, parenthesis and italics added).

Is there any reason you wouldn't want to receive Jesus Christ as your Savior and Lord right now? You can claim this prayer as your very own if you desire:

"Lord Jesus, thank You for dying on the cross to wash away my sins. I open the door of my heart and receive You as my Savior and Lord. Take over my entire life. Make me the kind of person You want me to be. Thank You for coming into my life and for hearing my prayer as You promised. I pray this in the name of my Savior and Lord, Jesus Christ. Amen."

If you prayed that prayer just now, you took the best "eighteen-inch" trip of your life. Congratulations.

Needless to say, you can see why I titled this chapter "The Eighteen-Inch Pitch." I use this pitch often. You can too.

Fourteen

THE HAPPY PITCH

After the experience with Lynda, the Lord showed me that following His lead is always best. God has a plan for everyone we meet. He wants us to realize this and to ask Him this question: "Lord, how far along are You with this person I'm talking with?" He then wants us to observe the person, much like a fruit inspector inspects the fruit to see if it's ready to pick.

How do you determine if the person you are talking with is ripe for salvation? You simply ask questions, knowing full well where you are going with the conversation. Let me illustrate with an experience I had when a salesman came into my dry cleaning plant with a product to sell.

This young salesman was ushered back to my press and introduced himself and the company he represented. I noticed he had liquor on his breath, and his eyes were already a bit glassy. I thought that a bit strange since it was only nine o'clock in the morning. It reminded me of the Scripture verses when Peter was addressing the crowd about his followers who were being ridiculed, and he was defending them. Peter said in Acts 2:15:

"These men are not drunk, as you suppose. It's only nine in the morning!" (NIV).

What seems funny to me is that it sounds as if it would be normal for them to be drunk later on in the day.

This young salesman gave me an impressive pitch about his product. My wife had been used of God to teach me sales resistance. I told the young man that I wasn't interested in his product, but I did have a few questions for him if he had time. He said he did have time and told me to fire away.

I asked him how old he was. He said he was twenty-six. I asked if he had been in the service. He said yes. I asked if he was married. He said yes and told me that he had a six-month-old baby boy.

He then asked me why I was asking him these questions. I told him that I was interested in him and wondered if he would allow me to ask him just one more question. He said, "Sure."

I asked him if he was happy. He looked down and said he wasn't. I waited for him to look up, and when he did I said, "You are looking at one of the happiest people you will ever meet in your lifetime." I turned away to press another coat and just left him there to see how he would respond.

He said, "Wait a minute. Why are you so happy?"

I asked, "Do you really want to know?"

He said yes, and I told him it would take me at least ten minutes to explain.

I ushered him to a private part of the building and shared with him how he could know Jesus Christ in a personal way. I told him about the joy that he would begin to experience as he obeyed the Lord.

I took a tract from my pocket and asked if he had ever seen it before. He looked at it and said no. I told him that this tract was filled with Scripture verses from the Bible that would explain to him why I was so happy.

He said, "That little booklet made you happy?"

I said, "No, the little booklet explains who can make you happy and content in any circumstance."

He was motivated to see what was in this little tract. We went through the tract, and he prayed and received Christ as his personal Lord and Savior.

He then did a strange thing. He looked at me and told me that I had caught him off guard. That made me curious. I replied, "Off guard?"

He said, "When I would go to church, I would block out what the pastor was saying. I never expected the owner of a dry cleaning plant to tell me about Jesus. You caught me off guard."

I asked him if he wanted to give Jesus back to me. He said, "No, Jesus is the one I've needed all along." As he left the building he literally jumped up and clicked his heels to the right and then to the left. He really needed a "happy pitch."

I pray that this book is being used of God to motivate you to throw some of these same "pitches."

Fifteen

THE PITCH MADE TO ORDER

Many salesmen came into our dry cleaning plant. Bob, a dry cleaning solvent salesman from Decatur, Illinois, had been trying to sell me his product for about a year. He would drop in our plant at least once a month. I had been purchasing this same solvent from a company in Peoria, Illinois, and was satisfied with their product and service. Bob was persistent but not pushy. We had developed a friendship during this time even though I never bought his product. We always had a lighthearted conversation when he came in, and I looked forward to seeing him each month.

I had noticed that he was a materialistic type guy, enjoying the pleasures of this world. I wondered what it would take to get him talking about spiritual matters. The Lord showed me again how His timing is perfect even when we might not be ready. All He wants from us is to be available.

One day Bob came in with extra determination to sell his product. I was in a goofy mood and was joking with him. Finally he said, "Jon, please give me an order!" He was serious.

I acted serious, too, and looked at him and said, "Do you really want an order, Bob?"

He said, "Yes!"

I said, "Are you sure you really want me to give you an order?"

He said, "Yes, I'm sure!"

I said, "OK, I'll give you an order. Get out!"

Bob took a step back, and we both laughed. He said, "If I weren't a Sunday school teacher, I might have said something I shouldn't have, Burnham." We laughed some more.

In my heart I was completely surprised. He had seemed so worldly, and here he was telling me about being a Sunday school teacher.

Needless to say, the Lord showed me that even though my crazy statement was not the normal lead-in to a spiritual conversation, being available was all He wanted.

Bob's statement swung the humorous secular conversation into a spiritual one as the Lord led me to ask Bob, "Are you familiar with the *Four Spiritual Laws* that Campus Crusade for Christ uses in their college ministry?"

He had never heard of them. I suggested that he might want to use them in his Sunday school class as a tool for those who don't really know Jesus personally. I said, "Let me show you how easy this is to present to the kids in your Sunday school class."

As I was going through the presentation, I noticed Bob's increasing interest and concentration. I got to the two circles that depict two different lives. The circle on the left shows a person who has not received Jesus Christ into his life. The circle on the right depicts the person who trusted Jesus Christ to come in and take over the throne of his life. The arrangement and size of the dots in this circle look like a Swiss clock compared to the contents of the circle on the left.

Bob said, "Stop right there. That's me on the left, the non-Christian circle. Here I am teaching Sunday school, and I'm not even a Christian."

I said, "No problem, Bob. Do you know how to get from the circle on the left to the circle on the right?"

He wanted the circle on the right to represent his life. He wanted Jesus to be on the throne of his life.

We turned the page of the *Four Spiritual Laws* booklet, and I asked him to read the suggested prayer to see if it answered the desire of his heart. This is what he read:

"Lord Jesus, forgive my sins. I open the door of my life and receive you as my Savior and Lord. Take control of the throne of my life. Make me the kind of person You want me to be. Thank You for coming into my life and for hearing my prayer as You promised."

He read the prayer and said that it made sense and covered all the bases. I told him he could claim that prayer as his very own and could read it out loud to God right now if he wanted to. I told him that Jesus would come into his life. I had the privilege to stand there and be Bob's human witness as he prayed to receive Jesus Christ as his Savior and Lord.

I asked Bob what this meant to him. He said, "Next Sunday I'll be teaching Sunday school as a Christian for the first time. I know Jesus now. Where in the world have I been?"

I told Bob, "That's exactly where we've been—in the world." Receiving Christ gets us out of the world's mindset.

I thank God that He gave me the pitch "made to order."

Are you ready? God will use you!

Sixteen

THE AGE-OLD PITCH

I found that the age of the person you are pitching to makes no difference in terms of the pitch being effective.

Years ago I was standing in the back of my dry cleaning plant when a man by the name of Lymann Dragoo came in to sell me advertisement space for bowling programs. He and I had become friends, and I was happy to see him again. That day I realized that I had never thought to talk to him about his relationship with Christ. This was the second year he had come. God's timing is perfect.

I prayed and asked the Lord how I could get into a spiritual conversation with Lymann in a way that wouldn't turn him off. As I walked up to greet Lymann, the Lord answered my prayer. He gave me an idea of how I could get the conversation started.

As I shook hands with Lymann and exchanged greetings with him, I asked him if I could ask him a personal question. He said, "Sure, Jon, what is it?"

I thought it would be best to go to the back room of the plant so we wouldn't be interrupted. As we got to the back room I turned to him and asked, "How old are you, Lymann?"

He replied, "I'm sixty-six, Jon. Why do you ask?"

I was about thirty years old at the time so I said, "I'm asking because you are older than I am, and I'm curious about something. Has anyone, during those sixty-six years, ever asked you if you knew where you were going when you died?"

Lymann told me that no one had ever asked him that question. I said, "If anyone did ask you that question, what would you tell him?"

He said, "I would have to say that I don't know."

I took a deep breath because the Lord was opening this up, and I wanted to make sure I stayed out of the way. I said, "If you met someone who knew the answer, would you listen to him?"

He said, "I sure would. I have been looking for that very answer for the last five years."

I said, "If I had the answer, would you listen to me?"

He said, "Sure, Jon! What's the answer?"

I took the *Four Spiritual Laws* out of my pocket and asked Lymann if he had ever seen this booklet before. He had not, so I proceeded. I opened the booklet so he could see what I was reading. I read:

"Just as there are physical laws that govern the physical universe, so there are spiritual laws that govern our relationship with God." As I went through the presentation, Lymann was glued to those pages. He saw that God loved him and died for him, even while he was yet a sinner.

Jesus claimed to be the only way for Lymann to get to the Father (John 14:6). In John 1:12 the Bible states that we must receive Jesus: "For as many as received Him, to them He gave the right to become children of God"(NKJV).

The clincher for Lymann was found in 1 John 5:11-13 where it says, "He that has the Son has life; and he that has not the Son of God has not life. These things have I written unto you that believe on the name of the Son of God; that ye may *KNOW* that ye *HAVE* eternal life"(caps and italics added).

I asked Lymann if there was any reason why he wouldn't want to pray to receive Christ right then and there. Lymann chose to pray to receive Christ because it was indeed the desire of his heart.

The thrill of that moment was wonderful. At that point Lymann did something that no one has done in front of me before or since. He reached for his billfold and pulled out a five-dollar bill and handed it to me. I refused the money and told Lymann that what he had just received was a free gift from God. I joked and told him he could send me a check later if he liked. As he put his money back into his billfold, we laughed and rejoiced at the same time.

A year later Lymann came in to sell me more advertisements, and he had some interesting things to say. He pulled out of his pocket the well-used *Four Spiritual Laws* tract that I had given to him the year before. He said he had shared this with his wife and children. I was real encouraged to hear that. Then he told me that he had been in Springfield, Illinois, getting some ice cream at a local Dairy Queen. The man inside the Dairy Queen stuck his head through the little square window and asked, "Do you know where you are going when you die?"

Lymann said, "Jon, there's another one just like you running loose in Springfield." We laughed and had a great visit.

I never saw Lymann after that. He brought a real blessing to my life, and I'm sure to many others as well. Lymann was not too old to receive the wonderful "age-old pitch."

Romans 6:23 says, "For the wages of sin is death, but the gift of God is eternal life in Christ Jesus our Lord"(NKJV).

Let me encourage you to keep pitching to young and old alike.

Seventeen

THE DUST-OFF PITCH

I was learning how to share my faith with others. My baseball past and my youthful attitude were used of God to "launch" me into a very natural ministry with teenagers. Being part owner and manager of a dry cleaning business, I had the opportunity to hire teenage girls to wait on customers and teenage boys to help me with cleaning up and with the heavier chores around the plant.

One afternoon I was in the front office talking with a young guy who was working for me. A customer came in who was a minister of one of the local churches. In passing I asked him if he had ever seen one of the spiritual tracts I had in our tract rack. I didn't stuff tracts in people's clothes after we cleaned the clothes. I simply had a tract rack on our counter so that anyone could take a tract if they so desired.

I picked up this particular tract and handed it to this minister, thinking he would be thrilled that a businessman would be so bold and not be embarrassed to share his faith in this way. The pastor leafed through the tract, acted nervous, put the tract back in the tract rack and left, forgetting to take the clothes we had finished for him.

I turned back to the young guy working for me and said, "Isn't that interesting? He is supposed to get me excited about the things of God, and he left all shook up. He even forgot his clothes."

The young fellow looked interested to see what that tract was all about. There must be something pretty powerful in there to run the preacher off.

I said, "Are you interested in seeing what's in that tract, or are you too scared to check it out?" He said he wasn't scared and wanted to see what the big deal was.

We went to the back of the plant so we wouldn't be disturbed, and I went through the tract with him. The tract stepped us through a simple plan of salvation. I asked him: "Do you see anything in here that should scare anyone off?"

He said, "No! In fact it should make a person see the need to do what it says."

I said, "Can you see any reason why you wouldn't want to receive Jesus Christ into your life now?"

He said, "I want to do that. I have all kinds of troubles."

Needless to say, the young man trusted the Lord Jesus Christ to be his personal Savior and Lord.

I told him that I was just a rookie Christian and had learned I needed to read the Word every day. I asked him to come in after school so we could go through the book of John together and get to know Jesus better. We met a few times, and he wanted to get his buddy in on this. His buddy was already a Christian.

The three of us got together, and it wasn't long before they wanted to invite a couple of girls they knew.

What was happening here? A teenage ministry was launched into being because of an interesting reaction from a minister to a gospel tract that simply explained the way of salvation.

Our ministry grew from the faithful few to as many as 250 teens in a given evening. They came from all over the tri-county area to hear this former jock talk about God in a way that they could understand. Many young teens became Christians, and several are on the mission field today. They memorized Scripture and lived the life. There were reports that during lunch at school, kids would yell across the cafeteria the name of a classmate who trusted Jesus as Savior in our home the night before. Those were exciting days.

I know God uses ministers. In this case God used a minister in a very unique way. God used that minister's strange reaction to bring about a ministry that continues to this day.

We thank God for that high inside "dust-off pitch." I guess we, and even a preacher, need to be backed off if we ever get in the way of the gospel. God used that pitch to start a whole new teenage ministry. I still feel like a rookie at times.

I hope you are enjoying the variety of pitches that God has thrown in this book. He has many more that I'll share with you. Have you ever heard of His "big buck pitch"? Please read on.

Eighteen

THE BIG BUCK PITCH

There was a young fellow named Tom who came to our teenage meetings where he received Jesus Christ into his life. After a period of time he grew in the Lord and wanted to invite his classmates to come to my home to hear what he heard about Jesus. Tom's classmates would have none of it. Tom was going to a private school, and his class had a special agenda. They said, "Tom, if you are so high on this Burnham guy, have him come here to our class and let him tell us what he believes on our turf."

Tom approached me with their suggestion. He said, "Jon, they won't come to your house like I did to hear what you have to say. They want you to come to their class and explain to them about Jesus and salvation. But, Jon, I've got to warn you about something. The class is called the 'Gestapo' class. The teacher gives the 'Gestapo' class permission to ridicule, embarrass and humiliate any guest speaker who comes in to see if he really believes what he's talking about. They feel that if they can get the guest speaker upset, it will prove that he's not genuine. They figure if he's not genuine, why believe him. If he can stand the heat, they will give credit where credit is due. Jon, since you are a redhead and light complected, your face gets red real easy. I've noticed that all you have to do is bend over and your face gets red. If it gets red during the time they try to embarrass you, I'm afraid they will think you're getting upset and will really nail you. Now, will you come to my class and tell my buddies about Jesus?"

What could I say? This teenage friend of mine had become a Christian through our ministry. I had the opportunity to show him that we can trust the Lord in any situation. This didn't mean that I wasn't nervous. I hadn't experienced anything like this before. There are times that the Lord will challenge us to step out in blind faith.

I said, "Tom, I'll be happy to come to your class. The Lord changed water to wine at the wedding supper in Cana. He can surely keep my face from turning red."

The time came to face off with the "Gestapo" class. These guys seemed harmless enough. The teacher was in the back row with a slight smile on his face.

Tom introduced me to the class. I stood up and told them that I would appreciate it if they would give me just five minutes without interruption so I could give my testimony. I said, "At the conclusion of my testimony you may ask me any question or make any comments you like. I do understand how this class operates."

During my five-minute testimony about my personal relationship with Jesus Christ, they listened without saying a word. When I finished a fellow in the back row stood on his chair and said, "I don't believe in heaven." The class roared their approval. He continued, "I don't believe in hell." Again they approved with applause. He continued, "I don't believe in the Bible." This time they gave him a standing ovation.

It didn't take me any time at all to realize that they were true to their reputation. These guys wanted to get me upset. The young man's comments proved that he had ignored my testimony completely, and the whole class agreed with him. He had a look on his face that said: "What do you think about that, Preach?" It was obvious that I was talking to the leader of the class.

I glanced at the teacher, and he was thoroughly amused. Naturally, the class was waiting to see how I would respond to this "anti-God" statement. I looked at the young fellow standing on his chair, and I said, "This tells me a great deal about you."

One of the students in the front row said, "What does it tell you about him?"

I replied, "I can't tell you. It would embarrass him in front of the rest of you, and I won't do that to him."

My answer caused a big moan of disappointment. I looked at that fellow in the back of the room again and said, "I'll be glad to tell you in private what it tells me about you. Come to the next meeting I have in my home, and I'll talk with you afterward. But for now, why don't you come up here to the front of the class? You seem to be the spokesman around here."

That got the approval of everyone. They all encouraged him to go up and face off with me. As he came forward—you guessed it—they applauded long and loud.

I asked his name. (Let's call him Bill.) I said, "Bill, what would you say you were?"

He replied, "I'm an atheist!" The boldness of his reply brought the house down. He was going to eat me alive, and they loved it.

I asked, "Would you take a piece of chalk and draw a circle as big as you can on the blackboard, and we'll let that circle represent total knowledge."

Bill did as I suggested and drew a circle that touched all the borders of the blackboard. I couldn't have asked for a better circle. I asked, "How old are you, Bill?"

He said he was fifteen years old.

I asked, "How much of all that total knowledge have you picked up during those fifteen years?"

He took the chalk and made a tiny dot inside the circle.

I said, "You're an honest young man." The class thought that was cool. I said, "How much of that total knowledge do you think you will pick up if you live to be one hundred years old?"

He took the chalk and increased the size of the dot to the size of a dime.

I said, "You're not only honest, you're smart. Einstein didn't claim much more than that, and we all recognize how smart he was."

The class really liked that. Now I'm comparing their leader to Einstein.

I asked for the chalk back, and I wrote the name "God" within the circle but away from his mark. I asked, "Looking at the circle, is it possible that God could be outside your frame of reference even if you lived to be one hundred years old? Is it possible, according to this illustration, that God just might be in total knowledge, but you haven't picked up on Him yet?"

78

He agreed with me.

I said, "Then, Bill, you're not an atheist."

The class thought he had been dethroned, and they moaned in agony.

Bill looked back at me and said, "Then what am I?"

I replied, "An agnostic."

That sounded "anti-God" enough to the class. As far as they were concerned, their leader had been reinstated.

I asked, "What kind of an agnostic do you want to be?"

He asked, "How many are there?"

I said, "I know of two. The ornery agnostic and the ordinary agnostic. You see, the ornery agnostic says, 'No one ever knew, no one knows today, and no one ever will know, but it's possible that there is a God.' The ordinary agnostic says, 'I don't know if there is a God or not, but it's possible.'"

I asked Bill which one he wanted to be. He said he had lost the title "atheist," so he chose to be an ordinary agnostic. With that established Bill went back to his seat, being wildly cheered by his faithful followers as though he had won a great victory.

As he headed back to his throne, a little guy on the front row asked me to explain what salvation was so they could see it.

I pulled out my billfold. I took out a one-dollar bill and asked them what it was. They yelled, "It's a dollar bill!"

I said, "If someone came into the room right now and saw me holding the dollar bill in my hand, wouldn't they assume this dollar bill is mine?"

They all agreed.

I asked, "Have any of you ever worked for me before?"

They said they had not.

I said, "Then if I give this dollar bill to any one of you, it won't be because you earned it, right?"

Again they agreed.

Then I said, "I will give this dollar bill to anyone in this room who believes me, no strings attached. I just want to give it out of the goodness of my heart as a free gift to anyone who believes me."

All those guys in that room started to yell out that they believed me. I yelled back, "I hear you."

Many stood on their chairs yelling at me, trying to convince me that they really did believe me.

I yelled back, "I hear you."

Finally—you guessed it—running from the back of the room came Bill. When he got to the front of the class he snatched the dollar bill from my hand. He turned around waving the dollar bill above his head in triumph. As he ran back to his throne he kept yelling, "It's mine! It's mine!" All of his buddies were on their feet yelling and applauding.

When it died down, I looked at the little guy in the front row, and I said, "That's salvation."

I continued, "There is one big problem. He believed a puny man for a measly buck. Why couldn't you believe Almighty God for eternal life?"

The bell rang, and the class was over.

The Lord threw the "big buck pitch."

The Lord tells us that some plant, others water, but the Lord is the one who gives the increase. An increase did come shortly thereafter.

Get ready to spend a "big buck." You will reap eternal dividends.

Nineteen

THE IMAGINARY PITCH

This is an account of how the Lord gave the increase from the previous "Gestapo" class experience.

Several weeks later we were having our weekly meeting in our home. We were doing a Bible study of the book of Proverbs. This book addresses almost every situation a person can experience in a lifetime.

Over the years we watched teenagers come to our home from as far as fifty miles away and from more than twenty high schools in the area.

Most of the Morton football team were there this particular night. Nine out of the eleven starters were Christians. The meeting had already started, and I was explaining some things from the book of Proverbs.

About that time three top jocks came in late from one of the schools in Peoria. They squeezed in, sat on the floor and leaned up against the wall. They immediately started poking each other and goofing off. One of the middle linebackers from the Morton team stood up and said, "Knock it off. Burnham's talking!"

The linebacker's outburst got their attention. They cooled it and didn't say another word until the meeting was over. This explains why I seldom had discipline problems during my meetings. If anyone wanted to goof off, someone in the group stopped it from getting out of hand. These teenagers wanted to hear what the Bible had to say.

After we finished our study for the evening, these three latecomers came up to me and asked if I remembered a guy named Bill from the "Gestapo" class.

I said, "Sure. How could I ever forget Bill."

They said, "We're friends of Bill's brother. We heard that it tells you something about a guy who doesn't believe in heaven, hell or the Bible. None of us believe in heaven, hell or the Bible. What does it tell you about us?"

I asked, "Is this why you came here tonight?"

"Yes," they replied.

I asked, "Do you guys have an imagination?"

They looked at each other and laughed. They knew what I meant. They said, "Sure, we have an imagination."

I picked up a Bible and asked, "Could you imagine that this is God's Word?"

They agreed that they could, at least, imagine it.

I asked, "Could you imagine that this Bible is God's Word for just one week?"

They said they could.

I said, "Would you have to change the way you're living during that week?"

Again they laughed and said, "Of course we would!"

I said, "Then it isn't a case of your not believing that the Bible is the Word of God. You just don't want to change the way you're living. Even without reading it, you know instinctively that this book condemns the way you're living. The Bible talks about heaven and hell. You probably fear going to hell, and you think you're not going to heaven because you blew it. Saying the Bible isn't the Word of God is mental gymnastics. You played that mental game to free yourself up to keep on doing whatever you want. You say you don't believe in heaven, hell or the Bible so you won't have to be accountable to God. Just saying it doesn't make it so."

I asked the biggest of the three, "When did you put this Bible on the shelf?"

He said, "When I was sixteen."

I asked, "Do you still remember her name?"

He said, "How did you know?"

I told him, "When you lost your virginity, you knew deep down inside that what you did was against God's game plan. At that point you logically thought through to the wrong conclusion. You decided to continue to embrace the girl, so you had to put the Bible on the shelf. You found you couldn't embrace the Bible and the girl at the same time. The Bible convicted you, didn't it? You think if you don't believe in heaven, hell or the Bible that everything will be cool. The trouble is you can only lie to yourself for so long. The truth won't go away. You are still accountable to God whether you want to be or not. Are you ready to face the truth so you can be set free?"

This young man surprised me with his answer.

He said, "I can't believe what's happening here. The three of us came here tonight to embarrass you in your own house by disrupting your meeting. Some big dude stands up and puts us down. Here I am wanting to accept this Jesus Christ you've been talking about. What do I have to do?"

I turned to the other two guys and asked if they were thinking the same thing. Both of them said they wanted to trust in Jesus too.

Only Jesus could change the hearts of three young guys. Jesus took their wrong way of thinking and turned it into a desire to respond to the very *One* they wanted to ignore.

I asked them what changed their minds. They said, "What you are saying sounds real."

I told them that I hadn't sunk my buck teeth in on this until I was twenty-six years old and that they were way ahead of me by believing Him at their age. I complimented them on wanting to nail this down right then and there.

I took the time to go through the Scriptures with all three of them and answered their questions as we went. They were all very impressed with the fact that they could "know" before they died that they would go to heaven according to 1 John 5:11-13:

"And this is the testimony: God has given us eternal life, and this life is in his Son. He who has the Son has life; he who does not have the Son of God does not have life. I write these things to you who believe in the name of the Son of God so that you may know that you have eternal life" (NIV).

It was a real highlight in my Christian experience to see the sincerity of those three guys as they opened their hearts to Jesus.

Bill, from the "Gestapo" class, never did come to any of our meetings, but God used what Bill told his brother to cause these three to come and hear the truth that set them free. You know, freedom is not the right to do what we want to do. Freedom is the power to do what we ought to do.

Romans 6:11 says, "In the same way, count yourselves dead to sin but alive to God in Christ Jesus" (NIV).

To count yourself dead to sin is to imagine what really is true for the Christian—to imagine that the Bible is the Word of God is true for everyone.

God used His "imaginary pitch" to cause these three guys to see the need for salvation, to see the reality of Christ. You can use any of these pitches. They are scripturally sound, and you too may see God's increase.

Twenty

THE RUBY PITCH

My wife, Bev, was in nurses' training when I met her. You ask, "How did you meet Bev, Jon?" Thank you for asking. I was hoping you would.

I knew that the best place to meet a nice girl was in church. A friend of mine, Roger Monroe, asked me to go with him to a college-age meeting at one of the local churches, so I went with him. Guess who sat behind me? You're right. It was Bev. She began to flirt with me. I, being an ugly gorff, wasn't used to this kind of behavior being cast in my direction. I immediately thought this girl must be blind. On the contrary, she had been a cheerleader for Central High School and had actually cheered against me when Woodruff played Central in basketball. I had noticed her at those times in high school. Now here she was flirting with me? I thought she was sharp, so I enjoyed this attention. After the meeting, like any red-blooded American boy would do, I got her phone number.

I didn't hesitate to call the number at my earliest convenience. I was soon to discover that the number went to the switchboard of the Illinois State Mental Hospital in Bartonville. I said to myself, "Well, Burnham, that figures. She's not blind, she's crazy. No wonder she flirted with you."

They rang her room, and when she answered I asked her, "How often do they let you out of there?"

She laughed and seemed normal enough. Bev said, "Jon, I'm out here with other student nurses as part of my training. I'm not one of the patients."

We laughed. It has been a big joke ever since. When asked where Bev was when I met her, I enjoy saying, "In the mental hospital in Bartonville."

Our dates consisted of one laugh after another. I have often said that I laughed Bev into marrying me.

Because I met Bev in church and because she was so active, being the president of her youth group, I assumed that she was a Christian. You already read earlier why I thought I was a Christian at the time. I was born in the United States. How could anyone have thought such a thing? But I did.

Bev told me how she felt so helpless when she was the nurse for a terminally ill patient. She didn't know what to tell them. Many times she would be the one to come into the room of a patient who had just expired. She knew there was a heaven and a hell and wondered where the person went who had just died.

She tried to fill the inner void in her life with dating and being active in good things. The void remained.

She thought that when she married me the void in her life would be filled. The void seemed to enlarge. She thought having children would fill the void. Nothing filled the void.

This brings us up to the time in Bev's life when I had been a Christian for about two years. She had noticed some good changes in my life.

About this same time Bev's mom, Ethel, asked her to go to a Bible study at the Altorfers in Peoria, Illinois. This class was led by Ruby Thompson, a godly woman. Ruby is a walking Bible. She can quote whole chapters of Scripture.

Bev's mom had been after her for a long time to go to this Bible class where she herself had been growing as a Christian. Bev's mom offered to pay the babysitter if Bev would go. She even offered to take Bev to lunch and shopping afterwards.

This creative project worked—Bev went to the class. Ruby was explaining that the word Christian meant "Christ in one." Bev thought to herself, *That's what happened to Jon. He asked Jesus to come into his life. Jesus must be the reason Jon has changed so much.*

Bev realized she had never received Christ into her own life. She had a wholesome respect for Jesus but only as a historic figure to be admired. Ruby led this group of women in prayer to receive Christ. My wife prayed along with Ruby and trusted Jesus to be her own personal Savior and Lord.

After the Bible class my beautiful wife was all excited. She began to share with me many of the things that I had shared with her. All this was now real to Bev. Talk about a neat experience. With Christ on the throne of my wife's life and Christ on the throne of my life, we found that He does not war against Himself.

God had used the "Ruby pitch" thousands of

times in people's lives in many parts of the world.

Thank you Ruby Thompson for serving up the Lord's "Ruby Pitch" to my precious wife. Bev and I, along with so many others, are extremely grateful for the way the Lord uses you.

We all thank God for the "Ruby pitch."

Twenty-one

THE FRANK PITCH

efore we were Christians, ego was on the throne of my life and ego was on the throne of Bev's life. We noticed early in our marriage that ego will always war against ego. It had been hell on earth, so to speak, until we began to experience how great it was to have Jesus on the throne of our lives because He doesn't war against Himself.

We soon learned that we were in for a different kind of battle. When a person becomes a Christian, the Lord doesn't remove the indwelling sin or, as some call it, the lower nature. The Holy Spirit comes in to give us power over the indwelling sin. A battle takes place between the two. This battle is explained beautifully in Romans 7:18-23:

"I know that nothing good lives in me, that is, in my sinful nature. For I have the desire to do what is good, but I cannot carry it out. For what I do is not the good I want to do; no, the evil I do not want to do—this I keep on doing. Now if I do what I do not want to do, it is no longer I who do it, but it is sin living in me that does it. So I find this law at work: When I want to do good, evil is right there with me. For in my inner being I delight in God's law; but I see another law at work in the members of my body, waging war against the law of my mind and making me a prisoner of the law of sin at work within my members" (NIV).

Let me give you an account of how God empowered Bev to be used in my life to reach a cousin of mine for Christ. My indwelling sin caused me to resist Bev and the very Spirit of God.

Bev called me at the office of our dry cleaning business and told me about a letter we got from our relatives in Macomb, Illinois. The letter informed us that my older cousin, Frank, was dying with cancer. Bev called me because the prognosis was not good. It was September, and they didn't think he would last until Christmas. She naturally wanted me to share my faith in Christ with Frank. Neither of us knew if Frank was a Christian or not, and Bev had a godly concern for my cousin. She called and expected me to jump on the phone and try to find Frank and talk to him about Jesus.

We tend to remember the impressions people make on our lives from early on. For instance, I remembered being with Frank years ago when I was in grade school. While visiting relatives in Macomb one weekend, we were near Frank's home playing around. Frank was bigger and older than I was. He suggested that we go a few doors down where there was a beehive. Somehow Frank knew those bees and I didn't. He told those bees to get me. I started to run, and they came after me. From then on I didn't have a "sweet taste" in my mouth for Frank. I was just a kid, and he was just a big bully.

Why am I telling you all this? Here I was, a grown man in my early thirties, and I get this flashback. I figured that if my first thought about Frank was negative, his first thought of me would be negative too. I began talking to myself. I thought Frank would never listen to me even if I did contact him. I dismissed from my mind Bev's idea to call him.

An hour went by, and Bev called me again and asked, "Did you get hold of Frank yet?"

I didn't want to tell her the conclusion I had reached, but I did say that I didn't think he would listen to me. After all, I hadn't seen him in more than twenty years.

Bev called a third time, and I explained to her the struggle I was having with my thinking (my indwelling sin). She told me to pray about it.

I didn't feel like praying about it. I picked up a pen to do some paperwork in the office, and the pen popped out of my hand. I thought nothing of it. I picked the pen up, and it squirted out of my hand again. I carefully picked it up and started to make a note when my hand had a spasm, and the pen fell on the desk for the third time. Finally, I got the picture. I said, "OK, Lord. I quit right here. You have my attention. I have to be honest with You. Frank is not going to listen to me. I remember him as a bully. He probably remembers me as a little kid he picked on. I'm sure he won't listen to me."

The Lord, in His kind way, gave me this thought, *"Do you think he'll listen to Me? When you gave Me your life, that included your mind, will and emotions along with your mouth, voice and everything else about you!"*

I replied in prayer, "You are right, Lord. Forgive me for standing in the way with my sinful human reasoning."

I got on the phone immediately. Six calls later I found Frank in a veterans' hospital in another state. They put Frank on the phone, and this is how the conversation went:

"Hi, Frank. This is Jon Burnham, your cousin from Morton, Illinois. I had quite a time finding you. Do you feel like talking for a few minutes?"

He said that would be fine, and I asked him how he was doing.

Frank said, "I'm not doing so good. They don't have a room for me so they gave me a bed in the hall."

I asked, "What do the doctors say about your condition, Frank?"

"Their diagnosis is that I have cancer. They don't give me much time to live. They told me not to count on making it home for Christmas. I'm glad you called, Jon. I'm pretty much alone out here."

I said, "Frank, are you afraid to die?"

"Yes," he said, and he began to cry.

I told him that I used to be afraid to die but I wasn't anymore.

He asked, "How did you lose your fear?"

I replied, "The reason I was afraid to die was because I didn't know where I was going—to heaven or to hell. Now I know where I'm going so I don't fear death anymore. Do you know where you're going, Frank?"

He said he didn't know for sure. He said, "How can you know where you are going before you die? I want to go to heaven. I thought you just have to wait and see, and that's what scares me. My time is running out, and I'm just plain scared."

I told Frank that I would be glad to tell him the answer from the Bible if he wanted me to. God had prepared Frank to hear the gospel, so I shared with him the good news right there over the phone, with the Lord listening in on His wireless intercom.

Frank saw his need for Jesus to wash away his sins. It is interesting that a person doesn't have to live very long to realize that they have a propensity for rebellion against God. We know instinctively that we are sinners. God is faithful to get the good news to us, for He is not willing that any should perish.

The Scripture verse that settled it for Frank was 1 John 5:10-13:

"Anyone who believes in the Son of God has this testimony in his heart. Anyone who does not believe God has made him out to be a liar, because he has not believed the testimony God has given about his Son. And this is the testimony: God has given us eternal life, and this life is in his Son. He who *has* the Son *has* life; he who does *not* have the Son of God does *not* have life. I write these things to you who believe in the name of the Son of God so that you may *know* that you have eternal life"(NIV).

I said, "See how you can *know* where you are going before you die, Frank? See why I'm not afraid anymore? Having Jesus in your heart makes all the difference."

Frank prayed with me on the phone to receive the Lord Jesus Christ as his personal Lord and Savior. Frank cried tears of repentance and tears of joy all the way through the prayer.

I'm sure glad my wife was faithful to have Christ on the throne of her life to encourage me to throw the "Frank pitch." This pitch led to another pitch that I will tell you about in the next chapter. Frank did live to Christmas and a few months beyond. I'll never forget the touching experience of hearing Frank pray on the phone as God took away his fear of death with His "Frank pitch."

Twenty-two

THE UPSTAIRS PITCH

Frank went on into Glory a few months after Christmas. I wanted to attend the funeral, but because of circumstances beyond my control, I was not able to do so. We were able to go the very next day.

That next day I had Frank on my mind. I kept thinking of his family and those he left behind. Because I hadn't seen Frank in years, I wasn't sure how many children he had. All of a sudden I got the number *three* in my mind and assumed he had three children. I couldn't get that number *three* out of my mind.

I could hardly wait to see his family and relatives. This number *three* kept reminding me of his three children. My spirit was quickened even more since I wanted to talk with the children about their dad and about the conversation we had on the phone when he received Christ as his Savior.

I knew the Lord would give me, within that hour, what to say to the children. God's timing is perfect. All day long it seemed like I prayed for Frank's family every time I turned around. Late that afternoon I called home to see if Lee, Mark and Holly were home from school so we could head off to Frank's home in Macomb, Illinois.

On the way we stopped to get a bite to eat at a restaurant. As we waited for our food to come, I asked my family what they thought about the situation. They were glad that I wanted to explain to the children how Frank made a decision to receive Christ several months earlier. I told my family that I was so sure Frank had three children because I had this number *three* in my mind all day. I couldn't explain it any other way. I didn't know how old the children were. We were all sure that Marilyn, Frank's wife, would be encouraged that we could come and be with them even for a brief time this evening. We left the restaurant with everyone in high spirits, anticipating what the Lord would do during our visit.

We arrived around 7:30 p.m. Marilyn answered the door. We went in, and she called to her children. Two boys came into the living room. I waited a few minutes for the third child to show up. No more came in. I asked if she had any other children, and she said no, that Frank Jr. and Kenny were all she had. I was puzzled. I shot up a quick prayer to the Lord asking why the number *three* all day when there were only two children. I got an immediate peace of mind as if the Lord were saying, "*I'll explain it later.*"

The boys were very young. They didn't look to be

older than six and eight. I sat in a chair in front of them with Marilyn and my family circled around the living room watching and listening to what I had to say.

I asked if they knew where their dad was. The boys didn't know for sure. This didn't surprise me. One of the reasons I wanted to talk with the children was because I didn't think Frank would know how to share his faith in Christ before he died.

I told them about the conversation I had with their dad on the phone. I told them how he trusted Jesus to wash his sins away and how he received Jesus into his heart to be his Savior.

They lived in a multi-level home, so I tried to explain it this way: "When your dad would go upstairs, here at home, you couldn't see him, right? Even though you couldn't see him, you knew he was upstairs. If you went upstairs, you could see him. Trusting Jesus made it possible for your dad to go upstairs to heaven. You can't see him now."

I asked them again, "Now where is your dad?" They both replied, "He's upstairs in heaven."

I said, "Are you glad to know where he is?" They looked relieved, so I continued, "He trusted Jesus to take him upstairs to heaven so you would know where he went and so you wouldn't worry. Do you know what sin is?"

They looked at each other, and Frank Jr. said, "When you do bad things you know you're not supposed to."

I asked them if they wanted to trust Jesus to come into their hearts to wash away their sins so they could go upstairs to heaven when it was their time to go. They both nodded.

I explained, "Savior means Jesus will save you from hell and save you for heaven. *Lord* means He will help you down here until He calls for you to come upstairs. That may not be for a while, but that's OK. You both are young, and Jesus has a few things for you to do first."

They followed me in prayer to receive Jesus. Then I asked, "Where is Jesus right now?"

They both said, "In my heart."

I said, "That's right. The Bible says that He will never leave you. You did the same thing your daddy did. That's why you will go to heaven when God calls you to be with Him upstairs. You will see and be with your dad again. Are you happy to know all this?"

They were in tears, just like their dad had been. We hugged, and I prayed, and we left for home.

On the way home I thought about the number *three* again. I told Bev that I was still puzzled. I knew that God doesn't make mistakes, so why had He given me that number so clearly all day?

Bev said she knew why. She said, "When you began to pray with the boys, I saw Marilyn pray right along with you. Jon, there were *three* who responded to Jesus tonight."

My family and I will never forget the joy we experienced having seen what the Lord did. He knows the end from the beginning.

It sure was a heartwarming "upstairs pitch."

Twenty-three

THE SANDY PITCH

Bev and I were interested in learning more about how to share our faith in Christ, how to make transitions from secular conversations into spiritual ones. We went to the Lay Institute, held at the headquarters of Campus Crusade for Christ in San Bernardino, California.

We got there and discovered that there were no sessions on how to get into a spiritual conversation with a stranger. The emphasis that week was the power and the leading of the Holy Spirit.

The first day of the conference emphasized knowing the Four Spiritual Laws presentation from memory. Bev and I had already done that. They gave us a stack of religious surveys and told us to hit the beaches of Los Angeles. We got to the beaches and went through many surveys, and people prayed to receive Christ. We were all excited about that. That evening people got up during group meeting and shared exciting results.

The next morning we were taught about the Holy Spirit and how He wants to lead us by faith. To be filled or empowered by the Holy Spirit by faith will help a Christian stay off the roller coaster style of life by not letting circumstances control the emotions.

After that session we hit the beaches again. This time we knew we were filled with the power of the Holy Spirit, and the results reflected it. This was not a mental hype. This was the evidence of the Holy Spirit leading His people with His power.

Let me share a few examples. When Bev and I walked up to a fellow on the beach this time, we knew that this was a divine appointment. We went through the religious survey with this young man, and he was open to know more about God. People were not this open to us the day before.

I went through the *Four Spiritual Laws* with him, and I asked him if there was any reason he wouldn't want to receive Jesus.

He said, "I would want to do that, but I don't think God would have me."

I asked him if I could show him from Scripture that He would indeed receive him into His kingdom. He agreed to let me go through some Bible verses with him. I opened the Bible to John 6:44: "No one can come to [Jesus] unless the Father...draws him"(NIV).

I mentioned that Bev and I came all the way from Illinois. "Jesus is in our lives. No one comes to Jesus unless the Father draws him, right? The Father drew you to Jesus in us, and we are from Illinois. God brought us this far to draw you to His Son in us."

We then looked at John 6:37: "Him that cometh to me I will in no wise cast out."

"If He won't cast you out, don't you think He will take you in?" I asked. "What do you think of that?"

He immediately wanted to receive Jesus, and he believed Jesus would receive him.

Let me give you another example.

The day before we went up to a man waiting to get into a volleyball game. He listened to us and was polite but didn't respond to Christ. The next day, after hearing about the way the Holy Spirit works, we went up to another man waiting to substitute in a volleyball game, and all of the players came over to see what we were doing. Six of them prayed to receive Christ. The difference was that we believed that the Holy Spirit was doing the work instead of us just going through a spiritual exercise for God. The whole day went like that. Talk about excitement! That night during share time there was hardly enough time to tell all the stories. What a difference a day makes. No, what a difference the Holy Spirit makes.

The Holy Spirit's powerful "sandy pitch" is a joy to watch.

Twenty-four

THE SINCERE PITCH

The Holy Spirit keeps you sensitive to what to say on the spot. The following is an account of how the Holy Spirit didn't skip a beat when I had an unusual experience while sharing my faith on the beaches of California.

I had been watching a volleyball game when a fellow came out of the game looking exhausted. I approached him with the thought that he would not be going back into the game right away. He was breathing heavily and actually asked me what I was doing on the beach with a clipboard and a Bible.

I told him that I was taking a religious survey. I asked, "Do you want to help me out?"

He said, "Sure, why not?"

We went through the survey, and he answered all of the questions without any problem. I then asked if he felt he was satisfied with his present relationship with God. He said, "I don't see how anyone can say that they are satisfied with being good enough to please God."

I asked, "Would you like to know God in a more personal way so that you would know just what does please Him?" He said he would like to know more about that.

I opened the *Four Spiritual Laws* booklet and began to go through it with him. He made no comment during the presentation. I had the four laws memorized so I could quote and look to see if he was really concentrating on what I was saying. He had his eyes on those pages.

When I got through presenting Jesus to him, I asked if he had a personal relationship with Jesus. He said he only knew of Him. I asked him if he would like to have a personal relationship with Christ. He asked, "How do you do that?"

I showed him the prayer at the end of the booklet. I asked him if this prayer answered the desire of his heart right now. He said it did, so I told him he could claim this prayer as his very own and read it out loud to God. That way I could tell when he had finished the prayer. I would be his human witness that he did, in fact, pray the prayer.

He read the prayer out loud and then looked at me. I asked, "Did you ask Jesus to come into your life?"

"Yes, I did," he said.

I asked, "Were you sincere?"

"No," he said.

This is where the Holy Spirit came to my rescue. I wouldn't have known what to say at that point. I then heard myself saying, "Well then, pray it again and be sincere!"

He said, "OK," and prayed the prayer out loud all over again.

I asked, "Did you ask Jesus into your life and were you sincere?"

He said he did and that he was sincere this time.

I then asked, "Then where is He right now according to 1 John 5:10-13?"

He said, "In my heart and life."

I said, "How do you know that?"

He said, "On the trustworthiness of God and His Word."

I said, "You've got that right. It wasn't because I said He would come into your life. He said He would come into your life if you believed Him. He can't lie."

I asked if he was glad that I came along to share my faith in Jesus with him. He said he was. I asked, "Are you sincere?" We both laughed.

I went on my way rejoicing in the Lord to find that Bev had just led another girl to the Lord.

The "sincere pitch" goes on. I hope you are enjoying these pitches that can be used in your walk with the Lord. He will give you pitches that no one else has ever used. God has just the right pitch for you to use at any given time.

Twenty-five

THE FOREIGN PITCH

B ev and I went to the Los Angeles airport to head back home from a great week at the Campus Crusade for Christ International headquarters in San Bernardino, California. We knew how to share our faith in Christ with people we had never met on the Pacific beaches of California. What was it going to be like in the real world? Bev turned to me while we were in the airport and said, "Jon, this is the real world right here. We had the boldness to go up to people on the beach. Why would it be any different here in the airport?"

I was not so sure I wanted to go up to people in an airport and strike up a conversation about spiritual things. I felt that when we were at the beach people were relaxed and could throw sand in our face if they wanted, but here? They could call for the airport police to escort us away for being an annoyance. This is the real world. Bev wasn't daunted. She said, "Jon, we came all the way out here to learn what we did, and now we aren't going to use it in this 'real world'?"

Bev saw a woman who looked like she had just arrived from Japan. Now here was a real challenge. Bev didn't know if the woman knew English, and we both knew that Bev didn't know a single word of Japanese.

I sat down to observe how my wife was going to get into a conversation with this woman. I prayed that Bev would be encouraged with her first attempt to share her faith following our time in the Campus Crusade Lay Institute.

Bev didn't jump right in with the religious survey she had in her purse. She waited until she had caught the woman's eye and they had exchanged smiles.

Bev asked, "Are you far from home?" Bev was checking out if the woman even spoke English. The woman answered in broken English and asked if Bev was far from her home. The conversation continued until Bev got the opening to share why we were in California.

Bev asked the woman what her name was. She said, "Masako Fukamoto."

Masako was very interested that Bev and I would come clear to California to learn how to share our faith in Jesus Christ. She stated that He must be someone very important. Bev asked Masako if she would like to know why He was so important. Masako was "most" interested. Bev opened the little *Four Spiritual Laws* booklet and began to read slowly so her newfound friend could understand.

At the end of the presentation Bev asked Masako if she thought Jesus was important enough for us to come all this way to learn more about Him. She agreed that He was. Bev asked her if she had understood enough to trust Jesus to be her own personal Savior. She said, "Yes, I want Him as my Savior."

Bev said, "You would?" Bev was amazed.

The Lord can open a person's heart no matter where we are. Bev gave this new sister in Christ some special information that would help her grow in the Lord just as the announcement came that our flight was ready to board. That was a very special experience for both of us to have.

Hebrews 13:8 says, "Jesus Christ is the same yesterday, today, forever"(NKJV).

Psalm 139:1-10 says, "O Lord, you have searched me and you know me. You know when I sit and when I rise; you perceive my thoughts from afar. You discern my going out and my lying down; you are familiar with all my ways. Before a word is on my tongue you know it completely, O Lord. You hem me in—behind and before; you have laid your hand upon me. Such knowledge is too wonderful for me, too lofty for me to attain. Where can I go from your Spirit? Where can I flee from your presence? If I go up to the heavens, you are there; if I make my bed in the depths, you are there. If I rise on the wings of the dawn, if I settle on the far side of the sea, even there your hand will guide me, your right hand will hold me fast"(NIV).

I pray that these experiences of sharing one's faith in Christ will encourage you to know that the Lord has many special pitches for you to throw that we may never experience. You may have many a "foreign pitch."

Twenty-six

THE CLEAN PITCH

When Bev and I returned home from California, she jumped right back into being a wonderful housewife and mother. I went back to work in our dry cleaning business.

Being in this business also involves shirts and household laundry. We didn't have the machinery for laundry so I would service our customers by taking their laundry to Peoria. Nick Bourazak offered us his laundry service and did a good job of satisfying our laundry customers.

Nick had noticed that we had been gone for a few weeks and asked me where we had been. I told him, "California."

Now since I knew Nick, I knew for sure he wouldn't be all that interested in what we had been doing in California. Remember now, I'm back in the real world.

I felt that if the Lord wanted Nick to know what I had been doing in California He would keep the conversation going in that direction. Nick continued, "What were you doing in California?"

I stated that we had gone to a type of lay institute. He said, "What kind of lay institute?"

I saw that the Lord was going to bring this to a head so I wanted to make sure that I didn't take over. I said, "The kind of institute that helps us to explain to people about God without turning them off."

Nick said, "Really? Tell me what you learned."

I said, "It takes about ten minutes. Are you sure you want me to do this?"

He said, "Sure, tell me."

I pulled out the *Four Spiritual Laws* booklet and got all the way through. I asked Nick if he had ever asked Jesus into his heart and life. Nick looked depressed and said, "I would never be worthy enough to be able to receive Jesus. He wouldn't want me. I have done too many wrong things in my life, and now I'm too old."

It just so happened that Andre Cole was coming to Peoria to perform his magic act. Andre was a great magician who had given his life to Christ and was associated with Campus Crusade for Christ. He performed throughout the world. Hundreds of people had come to believe in Christ as God honored his presentation of the gospel.

Bev and I invited Nick and his wife to go with us to see the performance to be held at the Pere Marquette Hotel in Peoria, Illinois.

At the end of the performance I didn't ask Nick

if he had responded to Andre when he had given an invitation to receive Jesus as Savior and Lord. However, the next morning was my regularly scheduled trip to Peoria to pick up the laundry Nick had finished for me.

I asked, "Nick, what did you think of Andre Cole last night?"

Nick replied, "It was very interesting how he tied his tricks into a spiritual presentation."

I asked, "Did you respond to the call to receive Jesus last night, Nick?"

Nick said, "When I got home I asked Jesus into my heart at least fifty-two times, and I'm still not sure He's there."

I asked, "Do you want to make sure right now?"

He said he did, so I went through the *Four Spiritual Laws* with him again. I asked him if he thought Jesus would come into his heart right now. I said, "It isn't a case of whether you believe Andre or me. It's whether you believe Jesus that counts. *He said* He would come in. He can't lie. Will you believe Him?"

Nick said, "Yes!" Nick prayed right then and there, and received Jesus. He immediately asked me if I would get him a small New Testament Bible like I was using and mark special verses like I had marked mine. He then asked if I would talk to his son Jamel to make sure that Jamel was going to go to heaven too. I assured Nick that I would talk to Jamel.

He then said, "Jon, how can I be sure Jesus is in my heart?"

I asked, "Nick, how many years have I been coming in here?"

He said, "At least six."

I asked, "How many times during these last six years have you asked me to get you a Bible, mark it and talk to your son about Jesus?"

He said he had never done that before. I said, "Before what?"

Nick said, "Before I had asked Jesus into my heart."

I said, "Nick, where is Jesus right now?"

Nick said, "He's in my heart." Nick's doubts vanished.

Romans 10:10 says, "For it is with your heart that you believe and are justified, and it is with your mouth that you confess and are saved"(NIV).

God used what seemed like a "magic pitch." There was no magic about it. Man can perform his magic and baffle the people watching, but God doesn't need magic. He gives us what is plain to see and hopes that we will believe by faith what He has shown us.

Nick saw who was plainly in front of him. He put all the wrong that he knew he had done at the feet of Christ, and Christ washed all of Nick's sins away.

Romans 8:1 says, "There is now no condemnation for those who belong to Christ Jesus"(NIV).

The Lord washes our sin away with the "clean pitch" (His blood).

Twenty-seven

THE SHOCK PITCH

A year had gone by since Nick Bourazak had received Christ as Savior and Lord when I got an alarming phone call from Nick's sister, Nellie. She was extremely upset and sobbing as she told me Nick had died.

She took several moments to give me the details, and as I listened I was asking the Lord to comfort her and guide me as to what I could say that would give her hope. As we talked, it became apparent that Nellie's main concern was that she would never see Nick again. In her mind Nick was gone forever.

I asked Nellie if she knew that Nick and I had talked about the Lord many times this past year when

I brought laundry to them. She said she knew we were talking about God, but that was all.

Nick hadn't grown enough in the Lord to know what to say to anyone about his newfound faith in Jesus. In fact, one of the things that proved to Nick that he really was a Christian was that he wanted me to speak for him to his son Jamel about God. He wanted to make sure that his son was a Christian and to make sure that Jamel knew his dad was going to heaven when he died. I responded to his request and talked to Jamel with positive results. Nick was delighted.

At this point Nellie needed some assurance as to where her brother was spending eternity.

Let me back up right here and say that there was the human shock that comes with news like this, yet I can't explain the immediate joy I experienced when I heard that Nick was with Jesus Christ in heaven. The Bible says to be absent from the body is to be present with the Lord (see 2 Corinthians 5:8).

I was glad that God prompted Nick to ask me about our trip to California. Then the Lord prompted me to share with Nick the gospel of Jesus Christ. The Lord had prepared Nick's heart to respond to Jesus. Then God just happened to have Andre Cole scheduled to come to Peoria to give a performance one week later. God's timing is perfect. He simply wants us to "be in the way."

Now, here again, the Lord prompted Nellie to call me because He knew that I knew about Nick's conversion. What I didn't realize at the time was that Nellie didn't know Christ as her Savior and Lord. As I asked a few questions, I noticed that God had prepared Nellie to receive the good news into her own heart.

I said, "Nellie, you say that you will never see Nick again. Are you ready for some encouragement?"

She said, "Yes!"

I said, "Nellie, Nick received Christ into his life about a year ago. I bought him a Bible at his request. I spoke to Jamel about the Lord at his request. Nick wanted Jamel to know that he was a Christian and that he was going to heaven when he died. He wasn't grown enough in the Lord to explain his salvation to anyone just yet. He couldn't explain it to Jamel, to you or anyone else. Many others may wonder where Nick is right now."

I went on to say, "In my opinion, after having prayed with Nick to receive Christ, and by virtue of the changes in Nick's life over this last year, I believe Nick is in heaven."

I asked Nellie, "Have you ever trusted Jesus to come into your heart, Nellie?"

She said, "No, I haven't."

I asked, "Did you know that Jesus said, 'I am the way, the truth, and the life. No one comes to the Father except through Me'? (John 14:6 NKJV). That means you, Nellie. That means me. That means none of us can get into heaven apart from believing that Jesus died on the cross for our sins. You must personally accept what He did on the cross for you. That's what Nick did, Nellie. Is there any reason why you wouldn't want to trust Jesus Christ as Savior and Lord right now on the phone?"

Nellie cried and said, "Yes, I want Jesus."

As I led Nellie to Christ over the phone I knew that her fears were ended. I said, "Nellie, you will see Nick again. We won't have to wait very long either, for the Bible says in James 4:14: 'Life...is...a vapor that appears for a little time and then vanishes away' (NKJV).This is all good news, isn't it, Nellie?"

I went on to say, "Nellie, I'm glad you called. I think the Lord had you call because He knew that I would be happy to tell you about your brother so you wouldn't worry. He knew you were ready to receive Jesus into your heart. God sure is faithful, isn't He?"

Nellie thanked me for sharing this good news with her.

I saw Nellie at the funeral, and she was radiant. Jamel knows where his dad is. Jamel will see his dad in heaven.

Using an alarming phone call, the Lord threw a "shock pitch" that reached Nick's sister Nellie. There is no end to the variety of pitches the Lord uses to reach the very ones He died for. Can you think back to the pitch He used to reach you?

Twenty-eight

THE PHONE PITCH

I was in the back of the cleaning plant one day, and I got a phone call from the Book of the Month Club. At that time in my life I didn't want to get involved with something that would take me away from reading anything other than the Bible. It was my favorite book, and I didn't want to use my time reading much of anything else since I was a slow reader anyway.

The girl was waiting for me to come to the phone, and as I was walking to the front office I asked the Lord what I could say to her. Anytime you have a conversation with someone it could be a divine appointment. I'm sure it was the Lord who reminded me of that as I picked up the phone.

"Hello, this is Jon Burnham. May I help you?"

The girl said, "Hello, Mr. Burnham. I'm Sue from the Book of the Month Club. We know that many businessmen have relaxing moments by reading a variety of books. We would like to send you one book a month at a very low cost to you. Let me read off some of the favorite books on our list."

I was listening and waiting for an opening. She went down the list of book titles and read off about ten of the best books she had to offer.

I said, "I'm impressed. There is a book that you didn't mention. Can you look down the list of book titles and see if you have my favorite book on your list?"

She asked, "What book might that be, Mr. Burnham?"

I said, "The Bible."

There was a long pause. She said, "I've looked all the way through, and it isn't on the list."

I asked her to look again because it had been a bestseller for years. She looked again and came back with the same answer.

I said, "Susie, Susie, Susie—you have to be kidding. Have you ever read that book?"

She said that she had read some of the stories in it. She said she had heard more than she'd read. She said, "Everyone seems to have their own interpretation."

I said, "What have you heard about it?"

Sue said, "I heard that people walked around a high-walled city, and the walls fell down. That's all well and good, but how can that help me now?"

I said, "That's a good question. Is that all you know about the Bible?"

She said, "No. I know it talks about God and heaven. I really don't know very much about the Bible.

Since it isn't even on the list, why is it your favorite book, Mr. Burnham?"

I said, "I'm glad you asked me, Sue."

I went on to explain, "Sue, this book was written by holy men of old, inspired by the Holy Spirit of God and explains how we can have eternal life. Do you know where you are going when you die?"

She said, "I hope I will go to heaven. No one can know for sure, can they?"

I could tell by her sincerity and the tone of her voice that she was really interested. I told her I had the Bible in front of me and that I would read her some Scripture verses that explained what I was talking about, if she had a few minutes. She said that sounded interesting and would like to hear what I had to say. I had her write the Scripture references down so she could check them out for herself.

Do you want these same Scripture references? Good! Here they are: John 3:16; John 10:10b; Romans 3:23, 5:8, 6:23; John 1:12, 3:1-8, 14:6; Revelation 3:20; and 1 John 5:10-13.

I explained what each verse meant to me and why it should be important to her. When I finished I asked Sue what she thought of a book like this.

I asked her if these Scripture verses were helpful to her. She said, "I want Jesus in my life. I want to go to heaven." She continued, "Mr. Burnham, I'm so glad I called you. Here I was trying to sell you the book of the month, and you showed me, as you put it, the book of the ages. No wonder it's your favorite book."

I led Sue in prayer and listened as she gave her life to Jesus.

The Lord has used the "phone pitch" many times over the years in my own personal ministry. He says, "Faith comes by hearing, and hearing by the word of God" (Rom. 10:17, NKJV).

The next time you use the phone, remember, the Lord is listening on His wireless intercom and will help you with that call.

Twenty-nine

THE MODEL PITCH

I was in my office one afternoon when I got a phone call from my friend, Dan. Dan was working at a local business, and he told me he had a difficult situation to run by me. Dan said that Jim, a fellow with whom he had been working, came up to him that day and said that he had put a gun to his head the night before. Jim said he was about to end his life when, all of a sudden, he remembered how consistent and happy Dan seemed to be.

Jim told Dan, "You seem to have it all together. I wish I had what you have. If you can't tell me today where I can get what you have, I'm going to kill myself tonight." Jim went on, "You see, Dan, I have been living a rotten life for years. I can't stand myself anymore. I'm not worth anything. Where do I get what you have?"

It was at this point that Dan excused himself and called me. After Dan explained all this, I could understand why Jim was so desperate. Dan asked me if we could team up and explain the gospel to Jim after they got off work. We decided to meet at my home that afternoon.

Dan and his friend arrived about 3:00 p.m. Dan introduced me to Jim as we stood in the foyer. Jim looked around with a smile on his face. Just to see him standing there one would never suspect that he had a problem in the world. I ushered them into the living room directly beyond the foyer.

Jim sat on the couch that backed up against the window that overlooked our back yard. Dan sat in a chair facing Jim, and I sat in another chair across from Dan, facing Jim. The furniture arrangement will prove to be significant as this story unfolds. Only the Lord could have known in advance how important the seating arrangement would be.

I asked Jim to explain to us all that was on his mind and why he was so despondent. As Jim shared his tale of agony, I was thankful that he had chosen not to pull the trigger the night before. Jim told us all that he thought was important for us to know.

For the next half hour Dan and I took turns sharing our faith with Jim. I sensed it was time to ask Jim if there was any reason why he wouldn't want to trust Jesus Christ as his Savior and Lord right then and there. Jim said that he saw no reason at all why he wouldn't want to do that.

After Jim prayed to receive Jesus, I asked him if there was a particular Scripture verse that gave him the confidence to trust Jesus. His answer was encouraging to both Dan and me.

He said, "Well, I want to back up a little and put it all together. If Dan hadn't been a good example at work, I wouldn't be here in your home at all. As I stepped into your home, I experienced something I hadn't experienced before. I sensed a tranquil atmosphere. Everything seemed calm. I stood in your foyer and looked around wondering why it seemed so different. I figured that you had children who were not yet home from school. I thought they would come in and put an end to this calm I was experiencing.

"I went into the living room with you guys. As I sat there listening to you, my heart was agreeing with everything you said. As I was listening, and sitting where I was, I could see beyond you to the foyer. I saw three young kids. I assumed they were yours, Jon. The biggest guy helped the little girl off with her coat and then he hung it in the closet. The little girl patted him on the back, and she went into the kitchen. The two boys went upstairs. I was waiting for some wild music that would shatter the calm atmosphere, but it didn't happen. I heard music that was consistent with what I was experiencing.

"Right at that point you asked me if there was any reason why I wouldn't want to receive Christ. All this put together was very convincing. I saw it in Dan's life at work. I heard you both explain the Bible in a way I could understand. Then I saw how your kids treated each other and heard the music they played. It all fit together.

"There was no reason why I wouldn't want to trust Jesus. I prayed to receive Jesus into my heart. There was something missing in my life, and I hoped this would fill the void."

Dan and I had another word of prayer thanking God for revealing Himself in so many ways to Jim. His Word will not return void.

The "model pitch" is yours to use every day. Do you see others who are using this pitch? Tell them you like what you see, and that will encourage them.

Thank you, Dan, Lee, Mark and Holly for using the "model pitch."

Thirty

THE PENNY PITCH

One day an employee came into my office with the news that a woman was waiting in the outer office to apply for a job. I went out to meet her and noticed that she was a woman in her fifties. She looked like she hadn't slept in days. By the looks of her clothing I could tell this woman had real needs. I handed her an application to fill out and told her I would put it in my file for future reference.

After she filled out the job application, she asked to speak with me again. This time I looked at her more closely and noticed that her eyes were watering, yet she wasn't crying. Her hair was matted down, and she had sores on her arms and on her legs that could be seen below the hem of her dress. Her hands were discolored and shaking. I felt sorry for her. I thought no one would hire this woman. I thought I was being kind and humane just to give her an application to fill out. I didn't picture myself hiring her either.

She told me that she desperately needed a job. I told her that I would check where she had worked before, and if we needed someone in the future that I would review her application at that time.

At this point in the story we will refer to this woman as Jane.

At the time I was talking to Jane, I didn't know that a present employee of mine was about to join the armed forces. The employee told me about his desire to serve his country just a few days after Jane came in to apply for a job. This left me with a position to fill.

I checked with Jane's former employers and found that she had lost many jobs in the past due to drinking alcoholic beverages. She had been drinking for years. She had never married and had a savory past. All the data I gathered convinced me that she was not a person we should hire. If I did hire Jane, I thought I might jeopardize the relationship I had developed with the other employees. All this was simply human logic. Common sense is supposed to be good. You have to be reasonable in these matters, right?

By the reports I got, I figured I would probably never see Jane again since she had been so consistently inconsistent in taking and keeping other jobs on her résumé.

A few days went by and here came Jane. She wanted to see me right away. I came up to the front office and greeted her. She asked if she could have a job. I said that there was an opening coming soon, but I wasn't sure if she was the one to fill the job.

Jane reached into her dress pocket and pulled out twenty-three cents. She said, "Mr. Burnham, this is all I have to my name. Please give me a job."

The Lord, in His special way, gave me an idea. The thought was to drive her hot or cold. I knew just what to do.

I said, "Jane, if you worked for me for six months and found out that I was a communist, what would you do?"

Jane said, "I'd quit! I don't like communists. Are you a communist?"

I said that I was not.

She asked, "Then why did you ask me that?"

I said, "So I could ask you another question. If we trained you for six months to do the job and you quit for one reason or another, we would have wasted our time and yours, right?"

She agreed with me.

I said, "If you worked for me for six months and noticed that I talk to people about the Lord, what would you do? Would that make you want to quit?"

Jane started to cry. She said a friend had been telling her for a long time that she needed to get right with God.

I said, "Jane, how have you been doing running your own life? Is there any reason not to let Jesus prove what He can do for you?"

She said, "No, I need to get right with God. I'm so messed up. What would He want with me?"

I said, "Christ has been waiting a long time to show you what He can do in your life. Let me show you a few things from the Scriptures so you will know exactly what is going on. Who can run your life better than the one who created you?"

Jane was ready. God had prepared her heart after all these years. She was thrilled with 1 Corinthians 6:9-

11: "Do you not know that the wicked will not inherit the kingdom of God? Do not be deceived: Neither the sexually immoral nor idolaters nor adulterers nor male prostitutes nor homosexual offenders nor thieves nor the greedy nor drunkards nor slanderers nor swindlers will inherit the kingdom of God. And that is what some of you were. But you were washed, you were sanctified, you were justified in the name of the Lord Jesus Christ and by the Spirit of our God" (NIV).

I pointed out that she could reside in verse 11 where it states that the people in that verse *were* like that (past tense).

She could be sanctified—set apart—and justified—just as if she had never sinned. Only Jesus could do that for a person by taking their sins upon Himself at the cross.

Jane prayed to receive Jesus as her Savior.

I looked at her as she opened her eyes after praying, and I saw my mom's face. Same features. I didn't notice this before. God let me see her in a different light. I told Jane to wait in my office for a moment. I stepped out and asked Esta, my Christian seamstress, to come in and meet her new sister in Christ. Esta got up from the sewing machine and stepped into my little office. She took one look at Jane and threw her arms around this new creature in Christ and said, "Welcome home, Jane." What maturity I saw in Esta. What a beautiful smile broke out on Jane's face.

My wife came over to the cleaning plant to meet Jane. She took her to the doctor, and with medication Jane's physical condition cleared up in no time. Bev took her to Bible study, and she began to really grow in the Lord.

After working for us for a little more than a year, Jane died. Her body had gone through a lot over the years.

Before God took her home to be with Him, He gave us a very special experience pertaining to His power. We had a heavy load of cleaning on the Monday before Easter. Jane had been pre-spotting our first load to put in the dry cleaning machine. I pushed the button to start the pump that circulates the pechlorethylene fluid that cleans the clothes. The pump didn't start. No electricity was going to the pump. I looked inside the big box of ten fuses.

As I was looking in the fuse box, Jane asked what the problem was. I told her that I needed to pray because I wasn't sure myself. I prayed, and she said, "What did God tell you, Jon?"

I said, "He told me that I had better call an electrician."

She laughed and said, "I could have told you that."

I called Joy, the electrician. He wasn't all that *joyful* when I called him so early in the morning. He came over and pulled out his electrical device to check the fuses. They all passed the test. Joy handed me some big fuses and said that there must be a short in the machine somewhere. He didn't know anything about machines like this, and, besides, he said he had a house to wire that morning.

Joy was walking out the front door when Jane said, "What are you going to do now, Jon?"

I said, "I think it's time to pray again." I prayed. "Lord, You know what is going on here. We are as busy as we can be, and the electrical expert just left not knowing what to do. What would You have me do now?"

A foolish thought came to my mind. It was like He was telling me to do something beyond human reason. The thought was to replace one of the ten fuses in the fuse box. I reminded the Lord that the professional electrician had just tested all the fuses, and they all passed the test. It was as though He said, *"Replace one anyway."*

I asked, "Which one do You want me to replace?"

It was as though He said, *"It doesn't make any difference."*

I said, "OK," and turned off the main power switch. I picked up the pliers to pull out one of those big honkers. I pulled out the fuse that was closest to me. I pushed the new fuse in its place, turned on the main power switch and pushed the pump button. It began to whirl into action. It worked! Jane threw her hands up in the air and came back down, doubled over, slapping her knees with delight. I was beside myself. I can't explain it to this day.

The Lord delights to prove Himself to us. He wanted me to put my faith in what He prompted me to do even if it seemed to defy all logic. I don't have to understand it. It was a fantastic way to start our Easter season. Jane got a taste of the supernatural God that she had just recently received as her Savior.

All Jane had in her hand were a few pennies. The Lord Jesus used them to make Jane a spiritually wealthy woman. A "penny pitch." It doesn't make much difference what we have in our hands or our pockets. Who is in our heart is what really counts.

A penny for your thoughts.

Thirty-one

THE RECORDED PITCH

Working with teenagers has been a real blessing. I remember one evening I was encouraging some young teenagers to memorize a way to share their faith. I had memorized the *Four Spiritual Laws*. I encouraged them to choose what method or system they wanted. Some favor the Roman Road or the Bridge, and I'm sure there are other favorite ways to get the salvation story told.

This evening I was showing why it was important to memorize a way to explain the gospel. One sophomore girl told me that she was a good student and could read well enough and didn't have to memorize any given method. I got a tape recorder and prepared it to record. I asked her to read the *Four Spiritual Laws* to her friend while I recorded it, then we would play it back. She let me know that this would make her nervous. I explained that in a real-life situation she would certainly be nervous. This would simply set up a mock situation to test her reading while she was a little nervous.

She agreed to read the *Four Spiritual Laws* to her friend, in front of the rest of us, as though she were really leading her friend to Christ.

She was halting in her presentation; she was nervous. When we played it back, she was embarrassed. It really sounded bad. It sounded canned and as if she didn't believe it herself.

One of the reasons to memorize the salvation message is that it sounds like it's part of your life. It will show others that you really believe what you are saying. It puts the listener at ease. Both their eye and ear gates are open. This gives greater freedom for the Holy Spirit to do His work in their heart. When you have the message memorized, you can glance up from time to time to see if they are really following along. If you are concentrating on what you're reading, you won't be able to be sensitive to them as you speak.

I told the group that memorizing a way to explain salvation is extremely difficult since the enemy, Satan, doesn't want that to happen.

The next night at about eleven o'clock the front doorbell rang. This young sophomore girl was standing there with her girlfriend jumping up and down with excitement. I asked them to come in and explain what had happened.

She said, "Remember the other night when I did so poorly reading the *Four Spiritual Laws* to my friend here? I was so embarrassed I went home and worked on those laws until three o'clock this morning. Tonight was our Friday night football game. After the game we jumped into the car of another girl who hasn't been to any of your meetings. There were six of us in that car. I was in the backseat. We were all yelling and acting up. Then the driver yelled at us to be quiet. She said, 'Quiet down. This is how teenagers have car accidents. I don't want to have an accident and get us all killed. Besides, I'm afraid to die.'

"I looked up from the backseat and said, 'Are you really afraid to die?'

"She said, 'Everyone's afraid to die.'

"I told her I wasn't. All the other girls got real quiet. The driver pulled over to the curb and stopped the car. She turned around and said, 'Why aren't you afraid to die?'

"I said, 'Because I know where I'm going when I die.'

"She insisted that no one can know where they're going before they die. I told these girlfriends that not only do I know where I'm going when I die, but God wants everyone in this car to know the same thing. I explained that I could tell them, from Scripture, how they could know for sure where they are going when they die."

She said, "Jon, I started quoting from what I had just memorized. We came right over to thank you for encouraging us to memorize the salvation message. The driver of the car asked Jesus Christ into her heart tonight. I'm so excited I can hardly stand it."

I was happy, too, as the Lord was truly glorified that night.

The Lord "recorded" this pitch for eternity. I would love to hear the playback on that one.

Thirty-two

THE BULLY PITCH

I was in a strange city doing street evangelism when I saw a mob gathered around two teenagers who were squaring off to fight each other. Having no authority I hesitated breaking it up. Besides I was just plain scared. The law would come soon and do their job and that would be the end of it. I still felt like I could have done something but didn't. I worked with teens. Shouldn't I have had the boldness to jump in there? That was not what I called a perfect setup to witness.

A few days later I was in my office pondering the street scene, remembering the two teens squaring off to fight. That window of opportunity was gone, but it wasn't too late to do something in my own hometown. I was sure there were a few bullies in the local school who would fight at the drop of a hat.

I had several teen employees, so I asked them who would qualify as the "bully" of the school. Each teen gave me an immediate answer. They all picked the same guy. We'll change his name for obvious reasons. Let's call him Tom.

I was told that Tom would have his buddies hold a guy up against the locker, and Tom would clobber him. I was told that Tom was the MVP in football and everyone tried to stay out of his way. He wasn't a Christian by any stretch of the imagination. I thanked my Christian teenage employees for their input. The Lord wanted to show all of us that greater is He that is in us than he that is in the world (See 1 John 4:4).

He put a unique idea in my mind and gave me the boldness to carry it out. I asked my teenage buddies to start praying for Tom and me. I had never done anything like this before, and I wanted to make sure I wasn't doing this in the flesh.

I called the school and asked to speak with the athletic director. I said, "I understand this is Tom's senior year. I'm sure you would like to see him do even better in sports this year than last year." He agreed.

I continued, "I have a plan that won't take long, but I will need to have Tom come to my place of business after school one day this week. That means he will miss practice. Will you let him off if he wants to come and see me? I'm sure he will want to do better in sports too."

The athletic director agreed with me and didn't even ask what the plan was all about. He agreed to have Tom call me. After school that day I got a call from Tom. The conversation went like this:

"Mr. Burnham, I was told to call you—something about helping me in sports this year."

THE WINNING PITCH

I said, "Hi, Tom. Thanks for calling me back. You don't know me, but I have heard a lot about you. I understand you were the MVP in football last year. I also heard that you're a pretty tough kid. I want to meet you. I have something I want to run by you that will help you do even better in school this year. I would like for you to come to my office after school. I cleared it with the athletic director. This may sound strange to you, Tom, but do you think you could make it?"

Tom said, "Sure, I'll be there tomorrow after school. I can't come tonight."

Tom kept his word and showed up the next evening after school. I introduced myself to him and he took a seat in my office. Naturally, he was very curious.

I said, "Tom, I understand you have won a lot of awards during your first three years in high school. I also heard that you're a tough guy. Many students are intimidated by you, and you don't hesitate to punch a guy's lights out if he crosses you."

Tom looked at me with a smile on his face and said, "Where did you hear all this?"

I asked if I had heard right. He said that it didn't sound too good the way I put it, but the information I got was accurate.

I said, "It sounds like you have turned the school upside down. The teachers will not only remember you because of your trophies, but they will also remember you as a tough guy who caused a lot of trouble in the classroom and in the halls. Does it bother you that you will be remembered that way? Would you rather be remembered as a guy who did well in sports and turned the school right side up during his last year in school? Which way do you want to be remembered?"

Tom looked thoughtful and stated, "I want to be remembered as a good guy. I have this rotten temper."

I continued, "You will need help to pull this off.

136

I would go to school with you to help out when things come up, but I have a job, and I can't do that. I do have a Friend who can go to school with you and give you advice on the spot. He'll never lead you wrong. He'll help you in your classes, in the hall and in sports. Are you interested?"

Tom looked at me as if to say, "You are pulling my leg." He said, "Who is this guy?"

I said, "Do you really want Him to help you? Are you serious about wanting to change. If you aren't serious, it won't make any difference if He's with you or not—you won't listen to Him anyway. Are you serious?"

Tom said he really wanted to change. Again he said, "Who is this guy?"

I said, "His name is Jesus."

He looked down and said, "My girlfriend has been after me to check Him out, but I never have."

I assured Tom that without Christ in his life his success would be limited here on earth, and he would still end up in hell after all was said and done. I asked Tom if anyone had ever explained salvation to him. He knew that he had never yielded his life to the Lord before.

I told Tom that he didn't have to meet Him if he didn't want to. I told him I didn't want a Burnhamite on my hands. I wasn't going to talk him into anything. "What do you want to do, Tom?"

Tom said he needed help and wanted to do this now.

I took the *Four Spiritual Laws* booklet and asked if he had ever seen them before. He hadn't. I opened it and we started reading. At the end of the tract there is a suggested prayer. Tom prayed to receive Jesus as his Savior and Lord.

I asked Tom if I could see what kind of guts he really had. He said, "Sure."

I had two teenage girls working for me that day. They were surprised to see him come in. I called them into my office. I looked at Tom and said, "Tell them what you just did."

He looked at the girls and back to me. He sat there with a smile on his face and asked the girls, "Do you know who I am?"

They called him by name and indicated they knew he was the star in sports at school. He looked at me and said, "They know who I am." He looked cocky, but I knew he was avoiding the test to tell them what he had just done.

I looked at Tom and said, "It isn't easy, is it? Ask your Brother to help you."

He looked at the girls again and said, "I just asked Jesus to come into my heart."

The two girls were excited. Smiles broke out on their faces. They seemed to lose their fear of Tom when they realized that he had just become their brother in Christ. They congratulated him. Tom had his foot in the door to turn the school right side up.

The Lord did use the street scene in the other city. It sparked me to reach out to a young bully in our own hometown. The Lord had been preparing Tom through his girlfriend to make this all-important decision.

God has a great "bully pitch." Guys aren't all that tough inside. Inside and high is a good place to throw the "bully pitch."

Thirty-three

THE SMART PITCH

I was in my office one morning when I got a panic call from a dad who was having problems with his teenage son. He wanted me to talk with him. The dad was a Christian so I asked him if his son had talked with their pastor. He said his son wouldn't talk to any preacher anywhere. I asked why he had called me since he knew that I would end up talking to his son about the Lord. He told me that he had explained to his son that I had been a pitcher in the Baltimore Oriole organization. His son was presently a pitcher in one of the local high schools and said he would talk with me. The son said to his dad, "Burnham can't be all bad; he's a former jock."

I have found that the Lord has used my former pro baseball status as a foot in the door with all kinds of sports-minded people.

I asked the dad to tell me how serious the argument had been between the two of them. He said, "We had an argument that got so bad that my son said if he had a gun he would kill me on the spot."

I could see why the dad wanted me to talk to the boy right away. I agreed to talk with this young jock the next morning before school.

This young fellow, Bob, showed up, and we got right into what had ticked him off.

I said, "What's the deal between you and your dad?"

Bob said, "I hate my dad. If I had a gun right now, I would shoot him." He gave me some particulars to justify his problem-solving technique.

I said, "What do you call someone who controls your life?"

Bob said, "A god."

I agreed. I said, "Who is controlling your life?"

Bob said, "I'm in control of my life."

I told him that he was wrong. I told him that his dad was in control of his life.

Bob asked what I meant. I said, "Your dad has such control over you that he could turn you into a murderer."

I asked him why he would let a god he didn't even like ruin his life by turning him into a murderer. "Is that smart or is that dumb?"

Bob said, "That's dumb."

I asked Bob if he had ever heard about my God. He wanted to know who my God was. I said, "You have used His name a number of times. Have you ever lost a ball game?"

He said, "Sure, lots of times."

I said, "Then you have used my God's name."

He said, "What are you talking about?"

I said, "When you lose a game, you blast into the locker room yelling, 'Oh, Buddha,' don't you?"

He laughed. I told him I had never done that either. "The name you used was 'Jesus Christ,' wasn't it? I used His name in vain, just like you. It seemed to be 'cool' to yell out His name like that. I had a potty mouth that wouldn't quit. I'm sure not proud of it.

"After my baseball career was over, I found out that Jesus Christ is not a swear word. Jesus Christ is the Savior who is ready, willing and able to keep you from becoming a murderer. He can keep you out of hell, and He can take you to be with Him in heaven when you die. I would say that He is a good God, wouldn't you?"

Bob agreed with me. I told Bob that Jesus cleaned up my mouth and that He alone could help Bob right now if he wanted Him to. I asked Bob if he would like to have Jesus run his life. I said, "Who can run your life better than the one who created you?"

I asked Bob if anyone had told him how to become a Christian. Bob didn't know how to get right with God, so I went through a gospel tract that made it very clear. Then I trusted the Holy Spirit to do the work that He alone can do.

After Bob had prayed to receive Christ, he reconciled with his dad a short time later.

Bob's salvation experience was used to bring other members of the family back into the fellowship of the church.

I trust that Bob is being used of God to throw some of God's unique pitches. I'm sure one of them is the "smart pitch."

Thirty-four

THE POWER PITCH

One evening while leading one of our teenage meetings, I had a unique experience in relating to a young teenage girl. This was the first of many encounters with people who would need to experience a very special "power pitch" from the Lord Jesus Christ.

There were well over one hundred young people at the meeting that night. I was speaking on how they could have a personal relationship with Jesus; all they had to do was to trust Him with their lives, to let Jesus be the boss. I was praying that these young people would see that He could run their lives better than they could.

While speaking to the group, I noticed a young girl sitting on the floor in front of me, rocking back and forth the entire evening. I had never seen her before and thought that this was simply a personal quirk of hers, so I didn't let it bother me.

At the close of the meeting I asked anyone who wanted to receive Christ to stand up. They had been sitting on the floor, and it would be a difficult maneuver to struggle to their feet. To stand publicly like that would be a gutsy thing to do. They would have to put aside their fear of what others might think. Peer pressure not to stand up was very real.

It was very encouraging that night to see many teenagers rise to their feet to indicate they wanted to trust in Jesus. They followed me in prayer to receive Christ and came up to get material I had for them to help them grow in the Lord.

After I had dismissed the group for the evening this "rocking" girl came up and introduced herself to me. Let's say her name was Betty. She asked me if she could have what those other teens got tonight. I looked at the expression on her face, and I noticed it was blank, yet she seemed sincere.

I said, "Do you understand what they got?" She just looked at me with a blank stare.

I explained, "When a group hears a message like the one you heard tonight, some will understand and respond to Jesus. Some people, perhaps like yourself, will need more of a one-on-one conversation about these spiritual things before they can respond to Jesus. Is this what you're asking for?"

Again she just looked at me with this blank expression. Not knowing what else to do at this point, I explained to Betty what it meant to be a Christian. She was very attentive to every word I spoke. When I thought I had covered all the bases, I asked her if there was any reason why she wouldn't want to receive Jesus Christ into her heart. She again gave me this blank look. Since I had given a clear explanation to her from Scripture, I thought it was time to test the waters.

I said, "Betty, say, 'Lord Jesus.'"

Betty opened her mouth and made a guttural sound, "Jeeeeeeaugh."

Again I said, "Say, 'Jesus.'"

Betty squinted, her face contorted, and she tried but couldn't get His name to come out. From what she had already said, I knew she could speak clearly.

I said, "Betty, do you mind if I pray for a moment?"

She just looked at me with the same blank expression. I prayed, with my eyes open, "Lord, Betty can't say Your name. There is no other name under heaven, given among men, whereby we must be saved. I pray, through the authority of Your name and the power of Your blood, to remove any demonic control over this girl so she can speak Your name. In Jesus' name I pray. Amen!"

I looked at Betty and said, "Betty, say, 'Jesus.'"

Betty said, "Jesus." She immediately burst into tears. I had her repeat the name "Jesus" throughout the salvation prayer as she trusted Jesus as her very own.

Betty cried during the prayer as one released from bondage.

I asked Betty, "Where did you come from, and how did you happen to be here tonight?"

Betty explained, "My folks moved here from another state. They found out that I had been attending a satanic church. It really bothered them. Dad got transferred to Peoria to get me away from their influence. Dad didn't know that I had reached the level of a 'white witch.' Three more months and I would have been a full-fledged 'black witch.' I used to go to this satanic church and watch wealthy businessmen drive up in their big cars and brag about how successful they were. I was impressed. I was a junior in high school at the time. The satanic priest would be dressed in black and lead us in worshipping the devil. We were forbidden to use the name 'Jesus.' When I was really getting into my craft, we moved here. We got to Peoria, and my folks insisted I go to a good church.

"Last Sunday evening, Pat, from your group, came to our church to give her testimony. While listening to her I had the desire to get her to see where the real power was. I wanted to get her on drugs and get her to give her body to guys and worship the devil like I was doing.

"After that meeting I asked Pat where she heard all the stuff she was telling us. She told me about you and how you talk about God. I wanted to come here tonight to show her that you had no power. I rocked back and forth to put a hex on you to prove my power was greater so Pat would want what I had. When you told the teens to stand up, I knew that no one would. I had put a stop to any power you might have.

"When the teens stood up anyway, I felt defeated. I then had a desire to hear more about what you were talking about. I came up and asked you if I could have what they got, and I couldn't even say His name."

Betty and I rejoiced in the Lord. I showed her 1 John 4:4: "Greater is he that is in you, than he that is in the world."

Betty could see that she had believed a lie from the liar himself. Now she had Christ who is greater than the one who promised Jesus "all these things" in Matthew 4:9 if Jesus would bow down and worship him.

"Where sin abounded, grace did much more abound" (Rom. 5:20).

The Lord uses the "power pitch" to show us His glory. Not that He needs to show us, but to see if we will be obedient to James 4:7: "Submit yourselves therefore to God. Resist the devil, and he will flee from you."

Thank you for reading *The Winning Pitch.*

After reading this book, did God inspire you to pray to receive Jesus Christ as your personal Savior and Lord? Would you send me your name and address so that I can send you a special gift?

If you would like to have extra copies of this book, please write to me at:

Jon Burnham
1116 Brentwood
Morton, IL 61550-2646
(309) 266-7639

It is my prayer that you will want to tell others about how the Lord Jesus changed your life.

God bless you as you are used of God to throw His "Winning Pitch."